Macramé Book for Beginners

A DIY Instruction Guide to Craft 13 Stylish Modern Macramé Projects for Your Home Décor and More Plus Macramé Knots, Patterns and Tips to Get You Started.

By

Roxanne Poole

Copyright © 2021 – Roxanne Poole

All rights reserved

No part of this publication may be reproduced, distributed, or transmitted in any form or by any means, including photocopying, recording, or other electronic or mechanical methods, without the prior written permission of the publisher, except in the case of brief quotations embodied in reviews and certain other non-commercial uses permitted by copyright law.

Disclaimer

This publication is designed to provide competent and reliable information regarding the subject matter covered. However, the views expressed in this publication are those of the author alone, and should not be taken as expert instruction or professional advice. The reader is responsible for his or her own actions.

The author hereby disclaims any responsibility or liability whatsoever that is incurred from the use or application of the contents of this publication by the purchaser or reader. The purchaser or reader is hereby responsible for his or her own actions.

Table of Contents

Introduction 6

Chapter 1 9

Essentials of Modern Macramé 9

    What is Macramé? 9

    History of Macramé 10

    Uses of Macramé 11

    Benefits of Macramé 13

Chapter 2 18

Basic Macramé Terminology 18

Chapter 3 22

Macramé Tips and Tricks 22

Chapter 4 29

Getting Started with Macramé 29

    Tools and Materials 29

        Cord/Rope 29
        Beads 32
        Wood or Dowel 33

  Adhesive Tapes 34
  Scissors.. 34
  Pliers.. 35
  Knotting Boards 36
  Metal Ring or Hoops 36
  Measuring Tape.. 37
  Tape... 37
 Basic Macramé Knots and Patterns 37
  Lark's Head Knot 37
  Square Knot.. 38
  Spiral Knot 39
  Hitch Knot.. 40
  Berry Knot 41
  Double Half-Hitch Knot.. 42

Chapter 5 45

DIY Macramé Project Ideas 45

 Macramé Wall Hangers.. 45

 Macramé Plant Hanger 52

 Macramé Yarn Garland 57

 Macramé Fish-Bowl Hanger 61

 Macramé Tote Bag 67

 Macramé Necklace 75

Versatile Macramé Strap 83

Macramé Light Rope 88

Macramé Christmas Tree 95

Macramé Table Runner 97

Double Macramé Plant Holder 112

Macramé Feathers 119

Macramé Ornaments 127

Chapter 6 138

Common Macramé Mistakes to Avoid 138

Chapter 7 145

Macramé Frequently Asked Questions (FAQs) 145

Conclusion 150

Introduction

So, you want to learn how to make macramé designs?

Perhaps you are still wondering if there is a better way you can learn this age-long craft and how hard it is.

Guess what? That's why you laid your hands on this book, to take all the mystery away from this fun retro crafting trend called macramé. However, I need to be clear on one thing before we start;

"You can do this."

You may still have your doubts, though, but that's why I am here and the reason I wrote this macramé tutorial for you.

But first, what is macramé?

Macramé is a textile crafting technique that uses different knots to form its basic shape and function. This age-long craft has been in and out of popularity for many years. Nonetheless, macramé will always be around to some extent due to its practicality. And since this form of art has regained its popularity in recent times, artists and crafters are springing up innovative ways to take macramé past the basic wall hangings and plant hangers such as table runners and key chains, which can be made with your bare hands and some inexpensive supplies.

For a project to be considered a macramé, it must incorporate one macramé knot at least. In several cases, macramé projects are joined with several knots and in other cases, macramé elements can be joined with other techniques such as weaving or knitting.

This book will provide you with the resources needed to find your way to embrace this fun art. The cool thing is you don't have to be an expert to make awesome decor pieces for your home, accessories and more. But to be honest, it does look much tougher than it is.

By the time we are done, you will:

- Have a good grasp of the tools and supplies of the trade
- Know how to tie basic macramé knots
- Have beautiful DIY macramé decor for your home, accessories, and more to get you started

- Be able to add making macramé designs as part of your skills.

And so much more!

So, let's get right into it.

Chapter 1

Essentials of Modern Macramé

What is Macramé?

Macramé is made through the knotting of textile materials. Macramé was majorly used by sailors and was crafted in a decorative or glamorous way. The primary use was to prevent the handles of knives, bottles, and some parts of the ships from being seen. The major techniques of knotting macramé are done through the joining of half stitches, which usually exist in a square form.

Macramé has many kinds and Cavandoli Macramé is one of the numerous kinds. Cavandoli macramé has a pattern that is designed like a geometric weaving or free-form weaving. Cavandoli is a kind of macramé that is knitted in a single knot and a two-half-hitch knot. Macramé can be crafted for other purposes too; for instance, it can be used to produce leather and fabric belts, bracelets can also be produced via macramé. Macramé can likewise be used for general house decoration, jewelry, or ornament, to mention but a few.

History of Macramé

Historically, macramé was believed to be used first in Babylon and Assyria. They made use of it as a form of braiding and fringe-like plaiting. Macramé was also found on the stone statues. The Arabians made use of macramé in a manner that sufficed as a towel; they knotted macramé around the extremes of shawls and veils and also used macramé as a form of decoration.

The word macramé metamorphosed from the word Arabic word "macramia," which was used to describe a strip towel, ornamental fringe, or a veil that was embroidered. There are, however, some opposing views as to the origin of the word Macramé and its meaning. Some people have opined that macramé was used to describe knitted textiles coined from the Turkish word "makrama" which was conceived as a napkin or a towel. Macramé was used as a decorative hinge, and the Turkish used it to prevent flies from perching on camels and horses. The art of making macramé moved to Spain, subsequently Italy, and then all over the European continent.

The reception of macramé in England was at the court of Mary 11 sometime around the seventeenth century. Macramé grew to become widely known, especially in the Victorian era; majorly, it was mainly used to decorate homes and produce things like tablecloths, bedspreads, and curtains. Sailors used macramé as a side hustle then; they made it in some quantity and then sold it off when they arrived on the land, which led to the multiplication of macramé across China and the new world. Hammocks and bell fringes were made from macramé by the British and Americans in the nineteenth century. Belts were also made. The term square knotting, which is one way used to carve macramé today, was invented by the British and Americans.

Uses of Macramé

Macramé can be used for different purposes, as seen below:

- **Table cover or table runner:** As a matter of fact, this is one major use of macramé; people widely use it to decorate tables. There are varieties of macramé table cover available. You may wish to visit a macramé knitter who would specially craft a table runner that suits your taste, or you get one for yourself in an ornamental or accessory market; better still, you can make one yourself.

- **Plant holder/ hanger:** Are you looking for a perfect hanger where you can fix your flowers, either in your sitting room or bedroom? Macramé plant/ flower holder is the right choice. Macramé can be customized in a way that flowers and plants can be placed in, thereby adding more beauty to your home. If you are a beginner in making macramé and are confused as to what to produce, then try designing a macramé holder.
- **Handbag, purse, back bag:** Amongst many things that you can use a macramé for are purse, handbag, back bag. There is this fashion it adds to one's dressing and sense of belonging.
- **Making a hammock with macramé:** Sailors mainly use this. The surprising thing is that making hammocks with macramé was passed down to this generation by the sailors some centuries ago. For those who may not know what a hammock is, a hammock is a bed-like sling produced from canvass; it is usually hanged between two or more angles. They use it for sleeping or resting in most cases. The trim of a

hammock, most especially, is made from macramé.
- **Jewelry can be made using macramé:** Accessories, such as jewelry, can be made using macramé. You can make earrings for a special friend, and a neck chain too. Bracelets can also be made from macramé. There is a firm assurance that making an accessory using macramé would last much longer.
- **Straps, keyholders, etc.:** Straps are meant for holding cameras. Key holders and hand fans are other things that can be made using macramé.
- Cases for sunshades and your accessories can be designed using macramé, same with light holders—for instance, the rope used for hanging bulbs. Laptop bags and document files are some of the things that macramé can produce.

Benefits of Macramé

If you are a lover of macramé art, several benefits come with practicing this age-long craft, some of which are given below:

- **Relieves stress and helps your mental well-being**

Macramé has a comforting effect on the human mind. Concentrating on your macramé work gives you some level of positivity and calmness from stress. Macramé helps to form a meditative atmosphere where you are presented with yourself and your craft, thereby not giving you the room to focus on the stress. This, in turn, helps you to have excellent mental health.

- **Boost self-esteem and confidence**

After you conclude a macramé project, the thoughts and feelings you derive will positively add to your confidence level and self-esteem. The feeling that comes from the efforts you made to create an amazing art would boost your confidence and self-esteem levels.

Additionally, it will also boost your strength and push you to work harder than ever. Indeed, there are many things to be proud of after creating a wonderful macramé art.

- **Improves the productivity of the brain**

Gaining knowledge of macramé and making a macramé art stimulates the brain and makes it productive. More so, you tend to be much more conversant with your ability to concentrate, reason quickly, and learn.

Whenever you choose to learn a new skill, new neurons are made, and bonds between receptors and the brain cells are also strengthened. As a result, this makes it easy to think productively, thus, greatly improving your brain cells.

- **Motor skills development**

With the use of your hands, learning knitting patterns and implementing them can help improve the muscles in your arms, fingers, and hands. Also, it enhances your motor skills, i.e., the speed at which you make new macramé projects. This is satisfying and beneficial for the human body, mostly for those with injuries or disorders. Additionally, carrying out the macramé craft with your kids can improve their motor skills, which allows them to perform other activities without stress, such as writing. This is a perfect representation that motor skills development not only happens to adults but also children.

- **Creates healthy competition**

Staying at home for a long time can become boring and tiresome. Crafts and arts such as macramé can help reduce these sad feelings and create a healthy competition and challenge for your body and mind.

Macramé is a skill that can help you create a fun and healthy competition within yourself and the people around you. For instance, you will begin this craft as a beginner and move up all the way to make more exciting and amazing macramé patterns.

Although the process of climbing up the ladder might take some time, it is worth working toward attaining. Even after attaining the top in creating macramé designs, you still need to continue practicing and building your skills to maintain your expert level.

- **Heals the body and mind**

Macramé and other soothing art can help heal the body and mind, thereby boosting and increasing our physical and mental health, positivity. Individuals who suffer from fear, ADHD, depression, and other mental illnesses can endure and emerge from bad situations by engaging in macramé.

Reduced stress, a better concentration level, and a happy mood are some of the results of practicing macramé. Macramé induces a comforting effect because of its constant knotting and the high creativity that comes with it. Additionally, it also slowly entices you to concentrate and feel calm, stable and captivated. Having good emotions and positive feelings can form dopamine, which is capable of healing your physical body. According to research, it was recorded that patients with Alzheimer's and dementia could reduce their negative symptoms and behaviors when crafts such as macramé are practiced.

Chapter 2

Basic Macramé Terminology

This section is a compilation of several macramé terminologies to help you get familiar with the terms and definitions you will encounter in the macramé craft.

1. **ASK:** This is an acronym for Alternating Square Knots. ASK is usually used in macramé patterns because of the common use of square knots.
2. **Bar:** This is a sequence of knots that leads to an increased part in macramé design. Furthermore, half-hitch knots are commonly used to make a bar, and they usually run vertically, diagonally, or horizontally across the body of a macramé project.
3. **Alternating:** This represents tying a knot using one cord and changing to tie the exact knot using a different cord.
4. **Body:** A major part of the macramé project.
5. **Bundles:** A long line of cords that are combined in one place.

6. **Button knot:** A tight and attractive round knot.
7. **Braid:** Also referred to as plaits. They are formed by crossing multiple cords to make them weave against one another.
8. **Buttonhole:** These are vertical larks head knots used to make a loop to attach macramé pieces.
9. **Crown knot:** A special type of knot used in macramé. It is also referred to as a Shamrock knot because it looks like a flower when it is completed.
10. **Cords:** They are any fiber material used to make macramé designs.
11. **Crook:** These are the curled parts of a loop of cord.
12. **Double half hitch:** This refers to the process of tying two half hitch knots close to each other.
13. **Fillers:** These are cords that reside in the middle of a macramé project. Fillers are also called core cords.
14. **Finishing knot:** It is a knot tied to protect cord edges and stops them from separating.

15. **Fringe:** They are lengths of cord edges that are always left without knotting.
16. **Hitch:** It is a knot used to join cords to other objects.
17. **Interlace:** It is a pattern whereby cords are woven together and intertwined to connect different sections together.
18. **Knotting cord:** A cord used to tie the knots in a macramé project.
19. **Loop:** The circle part that is formed when two ends of a cord are crossed together.
20. **Netting:** It is a pattern of knots that have exposed spaces. They are mostly used to make items like plant hangers and bags.
21. **Plait:** Also referred to as braid.
22. **Segment:** A particular area of a design, cord, or knot.
23. **Sennit:** It means a series of similar knots created one after the other.
24. **Standing end:** The edge of a cord attached to a macramé surface and not for making knots.

25. **Vintage:** A knot, technique, or pattern widely used in the earlier parts of 1900.
26. **Scallops:** They are loops of knots formed along the ends of a macramé project.
27. **Square knot:** One of the most popular types of knots made by tying two cords against each other.
28. **Synthetic:** Artificially made fibers like nylon and polypropylene.
29. **Natural:** They are cords derived from wood, plants, or other natural items like cotton and hemp.
30. **Diameter:** Used to mean the cord width counted in millimeters.
31. **Bight:** Narrowly folded parts of the cord forced through other sections of the knot.

Chapter 3

Macramé Tips and Tricks

This section outlines numerous tips and tricks that will help you in your journey to creating exciting macramé projects.

1. **Learn everything about knots**

Before starting your macramé journey, you should ensure you learn everything about knots. Knots come in different forms and there are a variety of knots to choose from. If you know everything about knots, it would be easy to make different macramé projects without having any issues.

Some good knots to learn as a macramé newbie includes clove hitch knot and larks head knots. After learning the knot, you can first practice it on a clipboard before replicating it on the main macramé project.

2. **Endeavor to have a good pair of quality fabric scissors**

As mentioned in the tools and materials section, scissors are one of the pieces of equipment needed in making macramé projects. Not just regular scissors, but good fabric scissors to create amazing macramé projects.

In some cases, a lot of rope can be difficult to cut simultaneously and may get all wrapped up. If that happens, what do you do? To not struggle, you should endeavor to get a good pair of quality fabric scissors that will help you cut the difficult or troublesome ropes while making your project.

3. Don't give up too easily

If you are not getting things right at the beginning, it is important to remain committed. Giving up means you have accepted that you are not good enough to make macramé designs. This can be bad for your macramé journey because even if you decide to make any macramé project, it will turn out to be a disaster.

So, remain committed, continue practicing, and you will become a macramé expert before you know it.

4. Cut more cord than you will ever need

This is one of the best macramé tips every beginner should know and take into consideration. You wouldn't like to run out of cord when making a macramé project that requires more cord than you have cut.

Even though you think you may not need the excess cord you cut, it is still important that you cut more cord than you will ever need. This will save you from the stress of cutting another cord when you run out of cord while making any macramé project.

To make sure you don't ever run out of cord, you can simply measure your preferred cord length, multiply it by 4 and proceed to cut your cord by the multiplication results it gives you.

5. Read macramé books and articles

There are tons of macramé articles and books to read and get equipped with everything to know about macramé, including the projects that come with it. For instance, this macramé book comes very handy because it talks about several aspects of macramé, including several macramé projects you can try out.

Not only do beginners have to read macramé books and articles, but professionals are also not exempted because they need to keep on refreshing their knowledge on improving their expertise in macramé designs and in general.

6. Take breaks when needed

Regular breaks are needed in any craft because it refreshes the body and mind. If you are finding it difficult to do a particular macramé project right, you should endeavor to go on a short break.

Once you come back from the much-needed break, your body and mind will be refreshed to make the macramé project giving you a tough time.

7. Find a comfortable work area

It would help if you found a soothing and comfortable work area to make your macramé projects. For instance, your work area might be in your bedroom or a different room entirely.

Also, you can decide to stay on the floor, stand up, or even sit on the couch while making your desired macramé project. Regardless of which options work for you, ensure you feel comfortable and relaxed when making your favorite macramé project.

8. Get all needed equipment, tools, and materials ready

Can you go to the farm without tools and expect to harvest farm produce? Definitely no. So, when attempting to make a macramé project, ensure you have purchased or gotten all the needed equipment, tools, and materials ready.

You certainly would not like to stop making your macramé project because you don't have scissors with you. As much as you may want to improvise and use other means to get what you want, having the compulsory tools and materials for a macramé project is still very important and advisable.

9. Don't be scared to unknot and start afresh

If you are not happy about something or are not getting something right, it may not be a bad choice to unknot and start the whole process again. Doing so will allow you to practice relentlessly and develop your macramé skills.

Although unknotting and starting your macramé project from the beginning is time-consuming, it will give you a sense that what you are doing is near-perfect. In the end, you will be happy when you see your finished macramé project, not minding the excess time you spent working on it.

10. Practice knots with spare yarn or string

Before you commence your macramé project, ensure you first practice your knots with spare yarn or string. Do not use your main yarn or string because you will end up halting your macramé project to get another one.

So, when preparing to make your macramé design, ensure to get a spare yarn/string and practice your knots using any of them.

A Short message from the Author:

Hey, I hope you are enjoying the book? I would love to hear your thoughts!

Many readers do not know how hard reviews are to come by and how much they help an author.

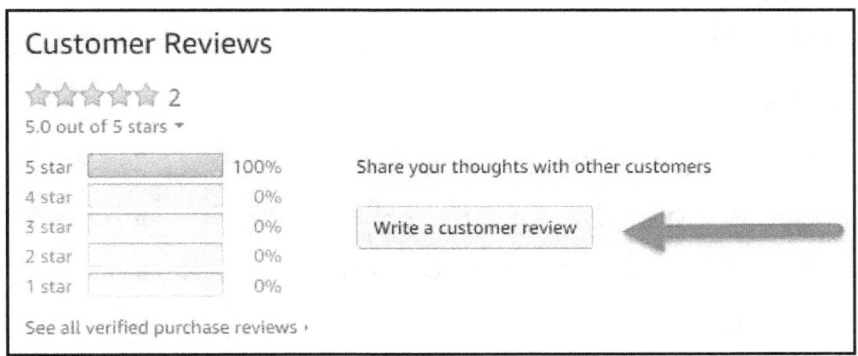

I would be incredibly grateful if you could take just 60 seconds to write a short review on Amazon, even if it is a few sentences!

>> Click here to leave a quick review

Thanks for the time taken to share your thoughts!

Chapter 4

Getting Started with Macramé

Tools and Materials

A concerted effort has been given to explain the uses of the tools and materials used in making macramé as shown below:

Cord/Rope

Most people don't know the various types of cords available. Good knowledge of this will help you choose a cord that will suit your design. Let's take a look at them below:

Macramé cords

A macramé cord is a group of fiber and strands which are twisted and braided together. They can be used to create knots or just tied together to form macramé. It is sometimes referred to as yarns, ropes, or strings. They all mean the same thing. Macramé cords are primarily found in a six-strand braid.

There are three types of macramé cords, which are:

- Braided cords
- 3-ply / 3 Strands
- Single Strands

Braided Cords

These are the type of macramé cords you will find in many stores and event centers, such as big-box retail stores, Wal-mart, Hobby lobby, et.c. People purchase it faster than other forms of cords because it is cheaper and easy to work with. The braided cord is made up of a combination of cotton, nylon, polyester, polypropylene and other fibers. Its major strength lies in its ability to hold objects and tie things together. It might have serious difficulties when trying to re-knot and fringe.

The braided cord is a good choice when starting your journey in macramé. The standard measuring diameter for macramé braided cords is 5mm, 6mm, 7mm and 8mm.

3-ply / 3 Strands

A 3-ply cord can also be called a 3-strand cord. It is made up of three small strands that form into a large twisted rope. When you hear the mention of three or four-ply cords, emphasis is placed on the number of strands twisted to form one single strand of cord. The Bochiknot macramé cotton cord has the following standard diameter measurement: 3ply, 4ply, 3mm, 4mm, 5mm, 6mm, and 7mm.

Single Strands

Single strand cords are more likely the best to use if you want to journey into macramé as a hobby or full-time work. They are more expensive than other cords. There are other inexpensive options like cotton cords. Whatever material you are using should be very flexible and comfortable to use. The single cords make cutting cords, tying and unraveling of knots much easier and faster. The macramé single strand cotton cords have diameter measurements ranging from three millimeters to seven millimeters.

Macramé ropes

These ropes are three-stranded ropes (also called three-ply) in which the strands are twisted around each other. There could be as many as four strands, but the most common is the three-strand ropes. A macramé rope is stronger than a string. It gives better flexibility when untwisted.

Beads

This is also an essential constituent of macramé craft. Beads also add to the beauty of macramé. When using a bead, make sure that you use big enough beads to go through the macramé ropes easily. If you want to add your beads to the macramé, just slide them either through the center of the knots or by the side. Always make sure that you go for beads that will match the pattern of your macramé. The various type of beads that you can use for your macramé craft are:

- Gemstone Beads
- Natural Pearls and Shells
- Glass Beads
- Wooden Beads
- Crystal Beads (Swarovski)
- Bugle Beads
- Crystals
- Delica Beads (Miyuki)
- Faceted Beads
- Seed Beads
- Rocaille/ Round Beads

- Shamballa Style Beads
- Lamp Worked Beads

Wood or Dowel

Wood or dowel are used to knit items or make a framed loom easily. Although one may use any other equipment that can suffice in place of wood or a dowel, wood or dowel are safe for adults and children.

Furthermore, wood or dowel are used for hanging things on the wall if there is any need to. Generally, the diameter of a dowel or wood is usually 1.2cm. One major advantage of a dowel is that it is convenient to use so that there is little or no discomfort while crafting your macramé.

A factor to consider while choosing dowels is the color. This only becomes an issue when the dowel is to be visible when the project is completed. Color choice is more of personal preference. Some people might prefer lighter colors while others deep and dark colors. Generally, wood or dowel can be gotten in different colors like black, redwood, walnut, and in its natural color.

Adhesive Tapes

They are primarily used for joining objects. Basically, adhesive tapes are made up of a material called backing or carrier, e.g., cloth, paper, plastic film, foam e.t.c. Some macramé projects would require the use of adhesive tapes to hold in place some decorative materials, e.g., beads. Adhesive tapes also protect the surface area of materials since there is no need to use extra fasteners to hold the materials together. It is more preferable to use them instead of liquid adhesives, which are more time consuming since they need to be sprayed or rolled on the surface before any bonding can occur.

Various categories of adhesive types exist from which you can choose from, such as;

- Pressure-sensitive tapes
- Heat tapes
- Water adhesive tapes

Scissors

At some point, while crafting, you will need to cut or tear apart fibers, cotton, and materials used to make a macramé. The recommended scissors for macramé are the Klasse-Heavy duty with Serrated Edge 210mm or Fiskers scissors. Although the scissors to use largely depend on individual preference, these types are good to get for your macramé project.

Pliers

The major use of pliers is for holding onto an object. Physically, pliers are described as forceps with matching, flat, and jagged surfaces. You can find some applications in gripping pipes and rods, while others can be used for twisting wires or even cutting some of them. You also require pliers for macramé crafting. Here you can use it to twist and cut some rods or even dowel parts. They come in different types;

- Side Cutting Pliers
- Long Nose Pliers
- Utility Pliers
- Diagonal Cutting Pliers
- Flat nose pliers

- Slip Joint Pliers
- End Cutting Pliers

Knotting Boards

Knotting boards are great to have while crafting a macramé design because you may sometimes have trouble holding knots and helms together, which can only be done with attachments made on the knotting board. Its use depends on the type of macramé project you are working on. You will most likely need them for more serious projects like wall hangers, suspended tables, and plant hangers.

Metal Ring or Hoops

They are bands that have a circular shape, used to bind a barrel. They can similarly be used to form a framework of any craft-making invention. For instance, you can use these hoops or metal rings to form a framework for a bracelet or earring.

Measuring Tape

Simply put, a measuring tape is used for measuring the length of the macramé cord.

Tape

This is used to tape the ends of the macramé cords. Painters tape is good because it is easy to remove. Masking tape is also recommended. You can, however, seal the cord's end by melting with a candle flame.

Basic Macramé Knots and Patterns

The different macramé knots and patterns are outlined below:

Lark's Head Knot

To create a lark's head knot, you need to, first of all, wrap your string in half, and this will create a loop. Subsequently, wrap the loop on the top of your stick to make the tails come in front and the loop appears behind.

Afterward, place the tails through the loop in the rear side, pulling it firmly to hold the cord to the stick.

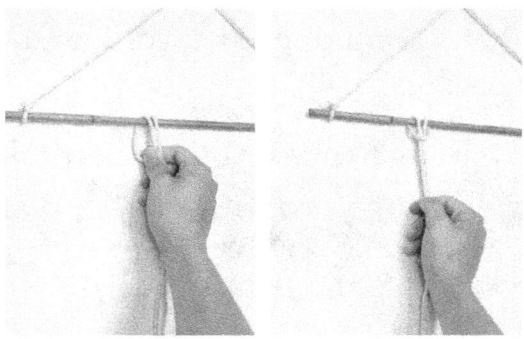

Square Knot

To make the square knot, you need to begin by joining two strands of cord, side by side, with the lark's head knot. For the square knot, you will only need the two exterior strands of cord and the two center strands will serve as the bottom part of your work.

You will create a "4" using the left strand of cord in the first instance, moving on the top of the two center bottom strands and below the far right-hand strand.

Subsequently, you need to pick up the far-right hand strand, placing or holding it on the top of the tail of the left-hand strand, and at the back of the two bottom strands, and through the "4" loop that the left-hand strand formed.

The next step requires you to pull firmly and go through the process once more. You are, to begin with the right-hand strand of the cord and not the left, creating a backward "4".

Lastly, pull firmly to make your perfect square knot.w

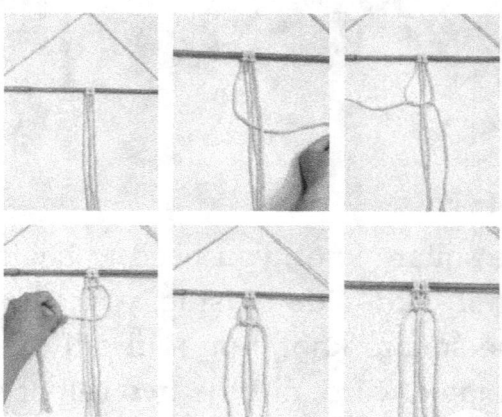

Spiral Knot

The spiral knot is nearly the same as the square knot but in a spiral form. You don't have to change the "4" pattern between the right and left strands. Instead, you will keep on working with just a single strand.

While moving on, pull the knots firmly, and from there, you will begin to notice that your work is spiraling.

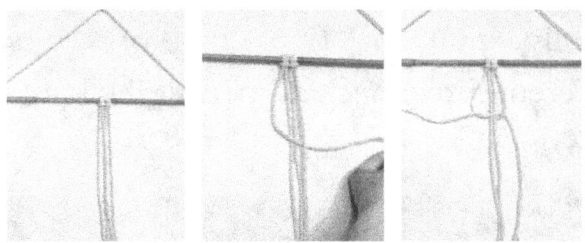

Hitch Knot

Hitch knots are used to tie a piece of rope to a stick or a fence. For the knot to stay intact without moving, it makes use of friction. Whenever you pull one edge of the rope, it also pulls the second end of the rope in another direction, making the knot much tighter.

Check below for the steps to tie a hitch knot:

1. Obtain some cordage or rope alongside a stick or post.
2. Fold the cord or rope around the stick/post.
3. Cross the cord on its body.
4. Proceed to fold the cord around the stick/post once more.
5. Also, place the other end of the string below the crossed string. This will make them go parallel in different directions.

6. Finally, pull the two ends of the strings in different directions and permit the knot to doddle down.

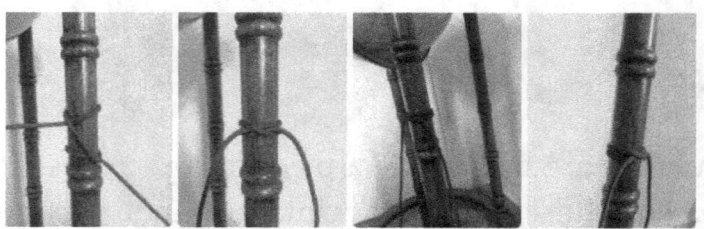

Berry Knot

The berry knot is a very attractive and decorative knot that is easy to make. The first step to make the berry knot is by making three square knots in a row. While doing so, ensure you leave a little gap above your initial square knot.

Subsequently, pick up the tails of your knots and loop them through the center of the gap you left on the top of your first square knot. Then drag the cord tails down at the back of your project, making a small berry ball with the line of square knots you made.

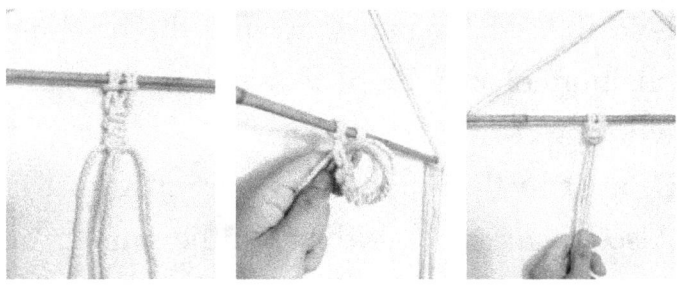

Double Half-Hitch Knot

To make the double half-hitch knot, you have to add some cords to your stick before actually making your macramé project. The knots are perfect for making lines in your macramé project.

Follow the steps below to make a double half-hitch knot:

1. Pick up the left strand and position it diagonally across the other strands using your right hand. This here will serve as your holding cord, while others will be your working cords.
2. Subsequently, pick up the other working cord below the holding cord in your left hand and further wrap it around the holding cord.

3. Fold the working cord around the holding to the position of the loop as well as the tail of the working cord.
4. Drag it to the upper part and ensure it is tight. Also, ensure you go through the same process by looping it around every angle of your holding cord.
5. At this point, you would have double loops around your holding cord, alongside the tail of your working cord which emerges from the center of the loops, from the back of the working cord.
6. Keep on with a similar knot on the next working cord, and similarly, keep your diagonal holding cord.
7. Halt the process of making the double half-hitch knot when you reach the center of your cords.
8. Go through the process of similar loop knots; however, at this time, you need to go diagonally to the left-hand side, with the right cord serving as your holding cord.

9. Keep on with the knots until you have exhausted the whole working cord.
10. Finally, you will make a final double half-hitch knot to attach the two parts, with the right holding cord serving as your main holding cord and the left holding cord serving as your working cord.

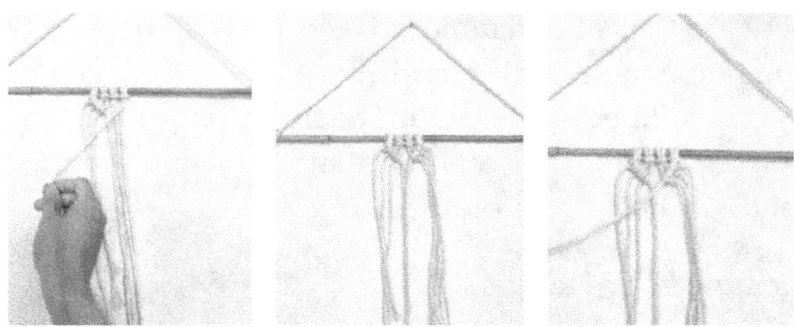

Chapter 5

DIY Macramé Project Ideas

Macramé projects usually come with tricky designs made using several knots, and they also have different sizes and shapes.

There are tons of macramé projects that can be made for your home, accessories, and more, and we have about 13 of them lined up for you. The interesting thing about these macramé projects is that they are beginner-friendly. Check them out below:

Macramé Wall Hangers

You can start your macramé projects by creating a wall hanger for your home. The process is straightforward and beginners can use this project to get their macramé journey underway.

Supplies

- Stick, Dowel, or Driftwood about 20 inches
- 188 Yards of 4mm 3 Strand Cotton Macramé Cord
- Scissors
- Measuring Tape

Instructions

- **Cut the cord**

In this step, you need to measure out and cut the needed cord for the project. On average, this step should take about half an hour and you are advised to cut the cord measuring about 28 strands.

- **Join the cord to the stick**

Subsequently, you need to join the cord to the stick, beginning with the 3-foot piece. This is needed because it will be used to hang your macramé project. To join the cord to the stick, begin by tying a knot onto a corner of the stick.

If you want to tighten the cord further, simply pull up on the longer side of the cord and tighten the smaller corner by pushing the upper loop down and pulling the little end tight. Thus, creating a tight lark's head knot. Finally, you can also do a similar thing on the other part with the other //cord end.

- **Make a triangle with square knots**

With the two attached cords and four complete strands, proceed to create a square knot. Keep on making square knots until you arrive at the end of the work. During this process, you can decide not to touch the first two cord strands. Then proceed to split the four strands from the initial square knot into half and use the first two strands of the second knot. From there, you will have two strands from each of the square knots, totaling 4 strands.

More so, you will also make a square knot underneath and in the middle of the previous knots. Keep on making the square knot to the end, but do not touch the final two cord strands. Furthermore, continue reducing by two on both ends until you have gotten the last knot below, forming a triangle.

The next step will be to do a double half hitch (DHH) along the triangle line to make an attractive triangle. The distant left cord will serve as the holding cord and you are expected to continue the DHH until you get to the center of the triangle. Your final DHH on the left-hand side should take half of the final knot in the triangle, while the remaining half will be utilized on the right-hand side.

Subsequently, DHH down on the right-hand side utilizing the distant right cord. After reaching the bottom part and you have exhausted the entire working cords, you should then use the right holding cord as the holding cord and the left one as your working cord. Make the final DHH and wrap up the triangle.

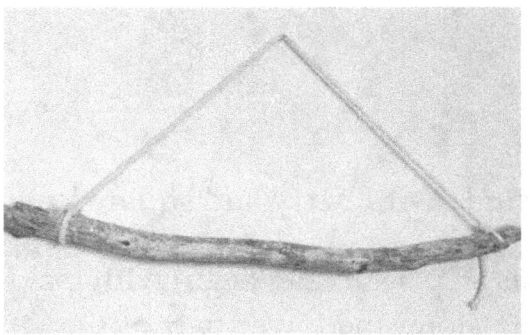

- **Make spiral knots**

Make a line of spiral knots heading down each corner of the triangle. Note that each spiral knot must have 10 knots. Meanwhile, on the right-hand side, make the spiral knots by creating the first side of the square knot with the "4" method. To make the right part spiral knots, you should make them spiral in the left direction, which can be done with the backward "4" method knot.

As a result, it will make the spiral move in another way. The next step is to close the triangle. You can do this by attaching two ends together.

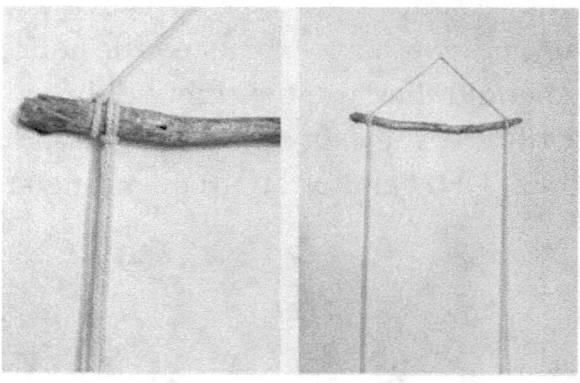

- **Conclude with berry and square knots**

To make this step a success, begin with making a row of square knots along the lower part of the DHH. For the small berry knots, locate the center and take two inner strands of cord from the two center square knots to create the berry knots.

Similarly, the subsequent four knots, seen on the left and right-hand sides, create extra two berry knots. In the end, you will have three berry knots in the center of the triangle. Finish the berry knots by using two strands from the left berry and another two strands from the center berry to make a square knot.

Go through the same process on the right-hand side with the two strands from the right and center berry. Additionally, with the new square knot tails, create a new square knot in the center. Then make the alternating square knot pattern without touching the two unused cords at the right and left ends.

Finally, conclude this macramé project by finishing this part with DHH on both sides and ensure the first knot is under the final row of square knots.

Macramé Plant Hanger

Macramé plant hanger is the ideal project for beginners during the sprint. With less than $2, you can make one and position it close to your window. Additionally, this macramé project takes about 15 minutes and does not require deep steps to make.

Supplies

- Scissors
- Plants in little pots
- Jute
- A tool to hang your plant hanger-on

Instructions

- **Cut the cord**

Like you have with other macramé projects, you will also need to cut the cord when making a plant hanger. Begin this process by cutting out 9 pieces of jute twine to your preferred size. It is advisable to begin with 100" pieces if you don't want the hanger to be long.

Proceed to fold the strings into hand and knot a little string in the center. Whenever you hold the strings by the little string, it will give you 18 pieces that have half lengths.

Lastly, hang the macramé project from a nail on the wall. This will allow you to use it without stress. Alternatively, you can also choose to work on this macramé project on a table, but it is better when hanging.

- **Make macramé braids and knots**

The next step will be to make macramé braids and knots. Start this process by cutting the 18 strings into three parts to form 6 strings each.

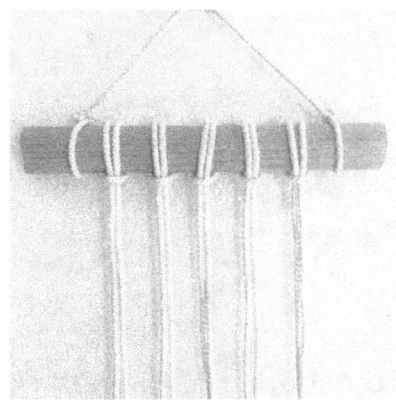

Then proceed to braid each part until you get your preferred length. To get an additional long plant hanger, you need to estimate about 24" length. Meanwhile, to get an average length, endeavor to braid 14" or thereabout.

- **Tie a knot at the corner of every braid**

Afterward, reduce or lessen from the braid knot about 6" or lower if you want to make a smaller one. Then cut the lower part of the braid in half to get 3 pieces on each side. Therefore, attach one braid to the closer one on the top by tying 3 from each braid using a knot. Go through the same process until the entire braids are joined.

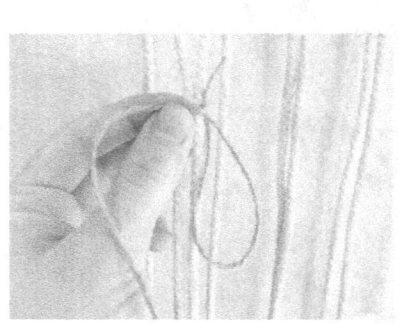 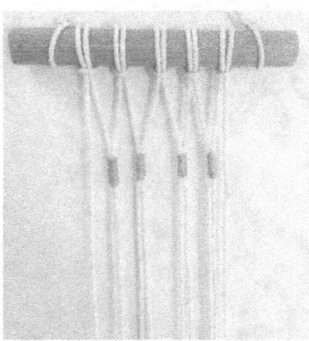

Also, reduce by another 6" or less and create a new row of knots.

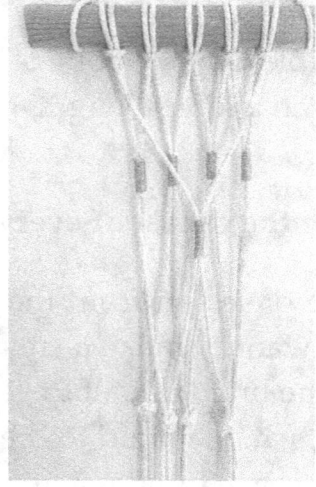

- **End macramé plant hanger using a large knot**

To end with, reduce it for the last time with about 6" and create a large knot with the entire 18 pieces.

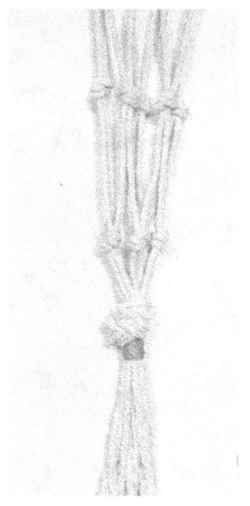

- **Cut or slice the strings a bit.**

Cut any excess string off and position the potted plant into the macramé plant holder to create your macramé plant hanger project.

Macramé Yarn Garland

The macramé yarn garland project allows beginners to get familiar with tying knots and getting involved with different colors. The exciting thing about this macramé project is that there isn't the involvement of excess materials, making it ideal for starters.

Supplies:

- Scissors
- Push pins or washi tape
- Chunky yarn (in different colors)

Instructions

1. Start by cutting one length of your chunky yarn for the bottom, depending on how you want it. Most people prefer to cut their chunky length about 8" long. Using your scissors again, also try to cut yarn lengths that are about 3" long, but it should be based on the amount of fringe you like to hang down. Don't get confused here because you can always return to this procedure to trim or cut them once again. You will have to get about

35 single yearn cuts to fit perfectly on this size garland in most cases.

2. Thereafter, hang your bottom strand to the wall using the push pins or washi tape and add the single pieces by tying one knot on the bottom.

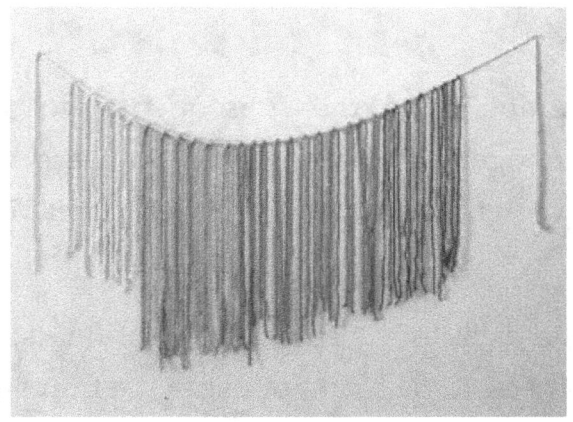

3. Begin the second row by moving past the initial yarn strand and tying two knots with the second and third strands. You can position it in the middle about 2" long down from the bottom.

4. Continue tying the subsequent two strands of yarn together and ensuring they are positioned between the knots on the lower yearn piece.

5. Move back to the second row of knots; however, you need to tie the knot using the first and second strands. Keep on tying the knot about 2" under the final knot. Once you have completed the second row, return to the left-hand side once more.

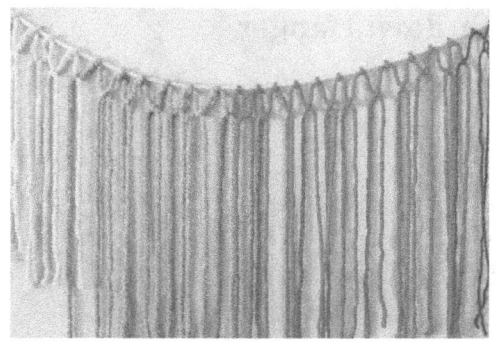

6. When you get to this step, you can either decide to halt your macramé project and conclude it or decide to continue the process using additional rows of knots. Meanwhile, this decision is solely yours and it is not compulsory.

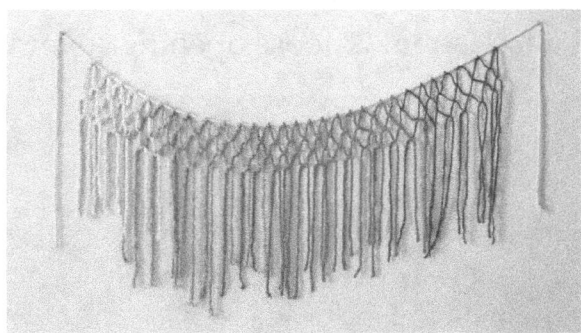

7. Regardless of of your decision, your final step is to cut down the ends of your strands to make them equal.

Macramé Fish-Bowl Hanger

Supplies

- Ceiling hook
- 50 feet nylon cord
- Scissors
- Plastic or glass fish-bowl

Instructions

1. First of all, you need to cut out 8 pieces of cord, each about 5 feet long. Then arrange the entire 8 pieces of cord and tie a giant knot at one edge, and allow about 2" loose openings over it.

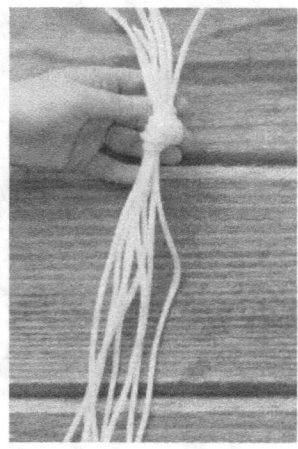

2. Divide the cord into 4 different parts, with 2 cord pieces in each part.

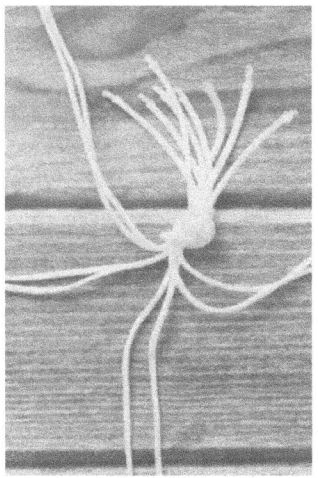

3. Take one of the parts and tie the 2 pieces of the cord into 2 knots, allowing a 2" space between the initial giant knot you earlier tied.

4. Go through the same process for the other three rope parts.

5. Pick up one piece of cord from the parts and join it with a piece of cord from the close part by tying

two knots 2" distance from the former knots you tied.

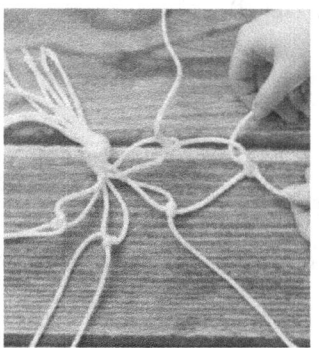

6. Duplicate this procedure for the other parts, with one piece of cord from the two separate parts.

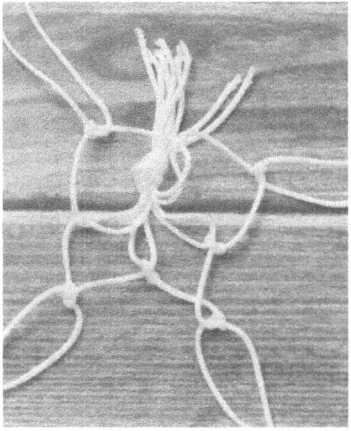

7. Repeat the last 2 steps above and take one piece of cord from the part and attach it with a piece of

cord from a close part by tying two knots 2" far away from the former knots you tied. This process should also be done for the other parts.

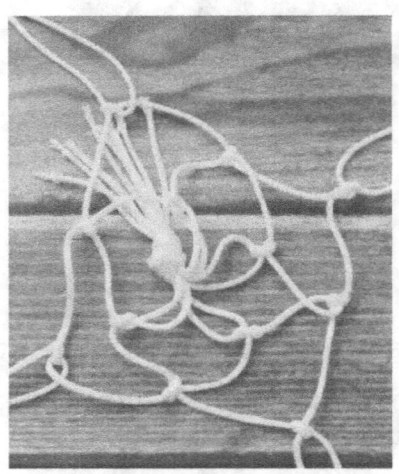

8. Position your fish-bowl over the knotted cords and on the first giant knot you tied. Proceed to pull the free ends of cords around the fish-bowl. As a result, the fish-bowl should stay on the knotted spot.

9. Subsequently, tie a knot joining the entire 8 pieces once more about 12" over the top of the fish-bowl. While doing this, ensure you allow for a sufficient gap to pull the bowl in and out for washing it. You can also tie a new knot at the edge of the open cords and pull it tightly, depending on how you want it to be.

10. Include a ceiling hook on the spot where you need the fish-bowl to hang. Then slip the hook below the upper knot, in the middle of the 8 pieces of cord. Ensure the 4 cord pieces are on

both sides of the hook. This is because it will hold the hanger right in a comfortable spot or area.

11. Place your fish into the fish-bowl and you have completed your macramé fish-bowl project.

Macramé Tote Bag

The macramé tote bag is a design that can be created for fun. It is also easy to make because the thread is thicker and the knots are much larger than other macramé designs.

Supplies

- Scissors
- Bag handles
- Jute rope

Instructions

1. First of all, cut about 10 lengths of 2.3-meter rope. Then fold the cut ropes in hand and thread the wrapped middle through the open space on the bag handle. Ensure you pull it tight and continue doing this process until you derive 5 pieces of rope joined to every bag handle.

2. Beginning at one edge, divide two pieces of rope and take the others to another side. In this process, you have to make the first knot using two pieces. This is the knot that will serve you all through your macramé project. Next, create a bend in the right-hand strand so that it goes on the top of the left rope at the right spot.

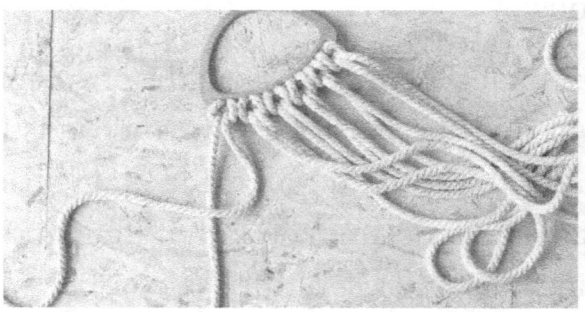

3. Pick up the left straight rope and thread it through the gap you created with the two ropes. Then pull the two ends of the rope far away from one another and do not stop until the knot has been created and it is in the correct spot. Depending on your preference, you can choose to make it about 5cm from the handle.

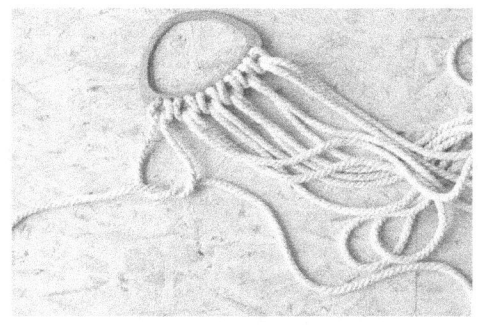

4. To conclude the knot, simply pick up the left-hand rope and place it on the top of the right rope. Proceed to thread the right-hand rope through space and pull the knot tight, allowing no space at all. At this point, you have made a finished double half hitch knot.

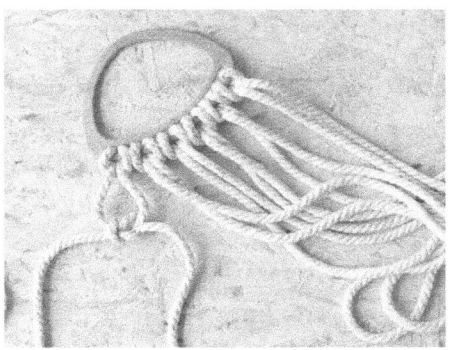

5. Create four extra knots in a row with the remaining ropes on the handle. You can begin

once more but go over the first rope and knot the subsequent ropes. Keep on moving along the row and create 4 knots but skip the first and final rope.

6. On completion of the second row, create the third row similarly as you did for the first row.

7. Once you complete making the third row, go rough the second, third, and fourth steps on the second handle. After doing so, take the two handles and attach them using the rear sides facing each other.

8. To begin the subsequent row, take two end ropes from the two front and rear bags and knot them together. Also, knot the ropes along the front and rear side until you get to the far end. Therefore, you would have only the last ropes on the back and front. Don't hesitate to knot the back and front ropes together.

9. Continue the knotting process in a similar pattern until you get about 10cm of rope on the left strands.

10. Then cut about 4 meters of rope and tie it on the final knot with a similar pattern that was effective for the handles.

11. Pick up a single strand from the front rope and another one from the back rope and fold the rope around them. After that, tie a single double half hitch knot and pick up two knots and perform the same process once more until you get to the end.

12. Undo the rope you find hanging and tie the strands of the ropes together between the knots to make them stay in one accord. Glue might be needed to make the knots tight. After adding glue, comb it and make a fringe to complete your tote bag.

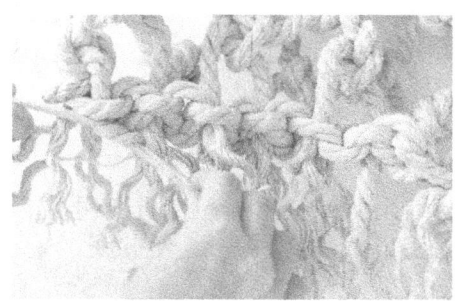

Macramé Necklace

Got a birthday party or anniversary coming up? Well, the macramé necklace can be the perfect craft design you can present someone with. The process is short and you can complete it in less than 2 hours.

Additionally, why worry about the cost of purchasing materials and tools when you can easily get them without breaking the bank.

Supplies

- Plier
- Scissors
- Rope
- Ring

Instructions

1. First of all, cut about 36 inch long strings from the rope. You can also use a fray check on the edges of the cut strings to keep them from unfolding.
2. Proceed to fold 2 strands of strings into half and make it pass through the ring you have.

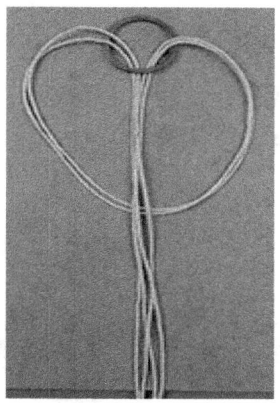

3. Go through the same step above for the other two strands. Ensure you follow them accordingly and not make any mistakes.

4. Using the outer strings, make sure you tie the first half of the square knot around the center of the two strands and pull them.

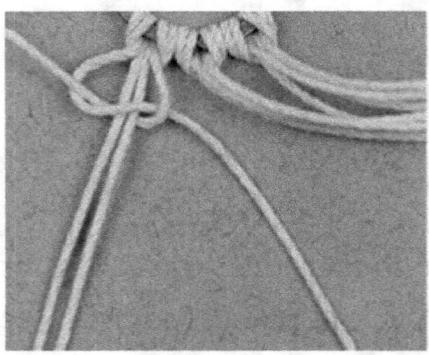

5. With the similar two strings, also ensure you tie the second half of the square knot and pull the snug as well.

6. For this step, repeat the previous two steps to create another square knot. This will serve as the

second one because you have previously made one.

7. Next, tie two square knots using the two unused sets of strings. Recall from the beginning that there were strings yet to be used. Take it up, and tie two square knots with the unused strings.

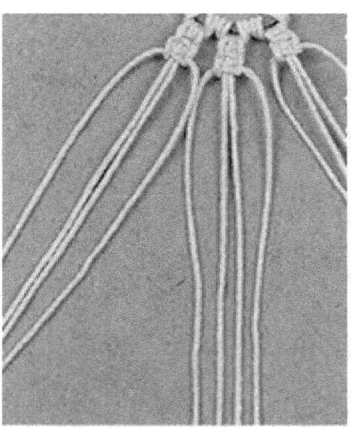

8. Proceed to divide or separate the strands and tie the subsequent row of square knots and make sure you allow for a 1" gap between each row.

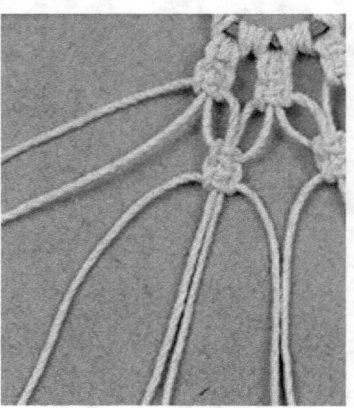

9. For the third row, separate the strands you find in the above step.

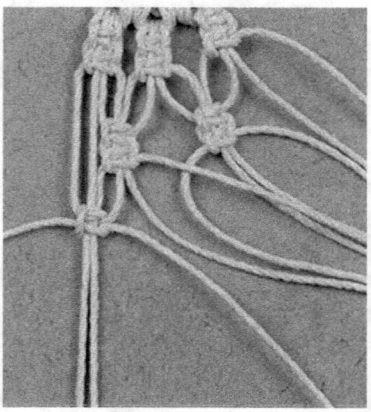

10. Allow 2" space between the rows and tie the subsequent row of square knots.

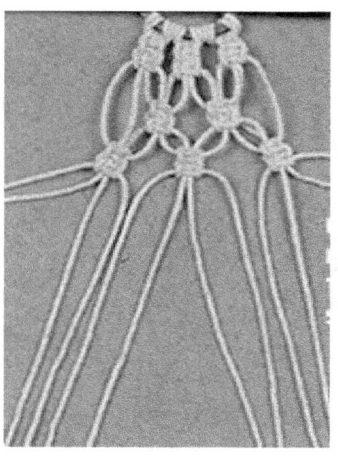

11. For the fourth row, separate the strands you find in the 8th step.

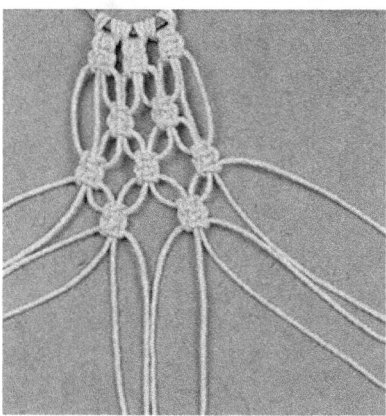

12. Finally, for the fifth row, separate the strands and tie the square knot with the four center strands.

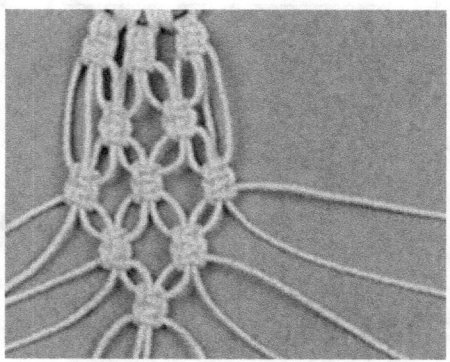

13. You are just about done with the process and you can place beads and tie them over the knot.

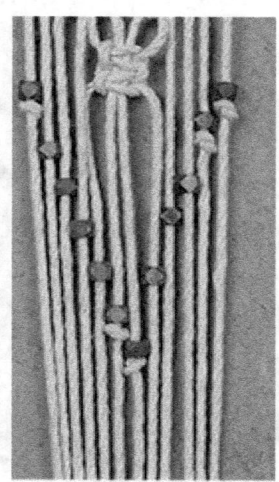

14. Try to open the large jump ring with your plier and join the macramé keyring to jump ring and turn to shift jump ring.

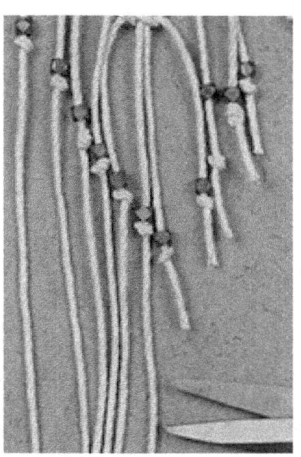

15. Lastly, get a chain with a little jump ring at an edge and a jump ring using a lobster clasp on another end.

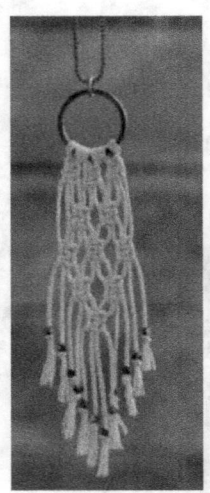

Versatile Macramé Strap

If you have a camera or item, you can make this versatile macramé strap for yourself. This macramé project will save you the stress of carrying your camera with the handle all alone.

Supplies

- Scissors
- Macramé cord
- Glue
- Clothespins
- Swivel clasps

Instructions

1. First of all, cut double lengths of macramé cord; this will make 4 yards.

2. Then fold each of the 2 cord lengths to make for one yard on one part and 3 yards on another side. Proceed to place the midpoints through the even side of one swivel clasp and making the long edges of the strands on the exterior part.

3. Pull the edges of every cord through its loop and pull the taut once more around the clasp.

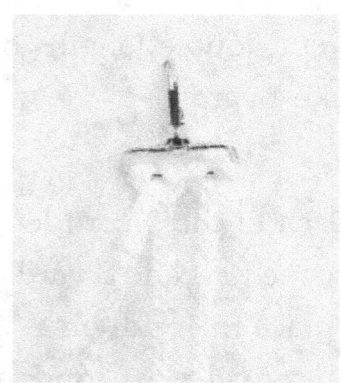

4. Start the next process by tying a square knot. Do this by taking the left-hand cord (it is the longest part), and move it on the top of the two middle cords and below the right-hand cord. Furthermore, take the right-hand cord and below the two middle and over the left cord. Then pull the taut and it will make for half of your square knot.

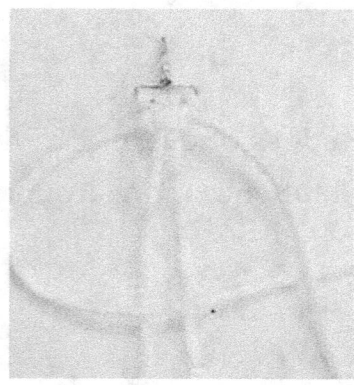

5. Conclude the square knot by making the reverse of the previous step. Go on to move it around the right cord on the top of the two centers and below the left part. While on it, move it to the left cord bottom two center and on the top of the right part. Lastly, pull the taut and you will get your finished square knot.

6. Keep on tying the square knots until the strap has gotten to your desired length.

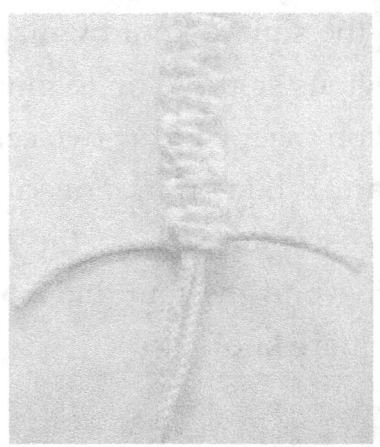

7. Cut the edges of the entire 4 cords and put the entire 4 cords through another swivel clasp. Position a dollop of glue on the edge of every cord, and fold the cords on the top of the clasp. Finally, hold the cord with clothespins and wait until the glue becomes dried.

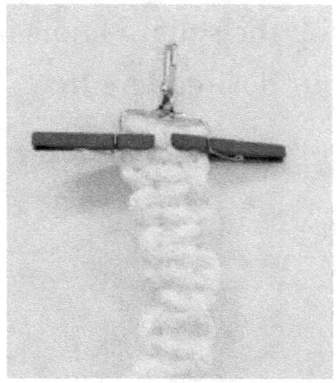

8. After the glue has dried, take out the clips, and you will get your strap for your camera or other items. The beauty of this macramé cord is that it is light, flexible, and can easily fit around your neck.

Macramé Light Rope

Is the festive period approaching and you want to make an attractive macramé design? Why not consider making a macramé light rope? The macramé light rope is used to hand bright lights for different events or occasions.

Supplies

- Rope
- Tape
- Cup
- Glue

Instructions

1. Acquire your lamp wire. You can either decide to tape it to a doorknob, a wall, or the back of a chair. As a result, this will make it stable.

2. Locate the middle of your cord and position it at the back of the lamp wire.

3. Pick up the left-hand part and place it on the top of the front lamp wire.

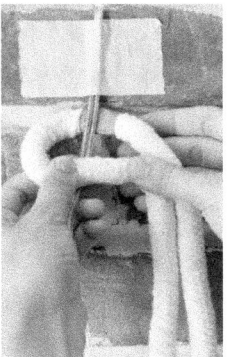

4. Below the right part of the cord, make a little loop on the left part of your lamp wire.

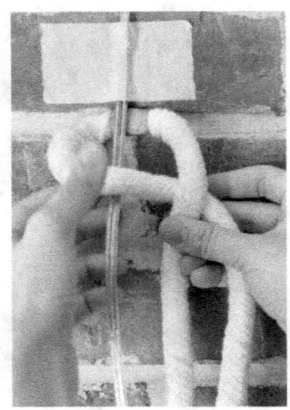

5. Also, pick up the right cord and position it at the back of the lamp wire.

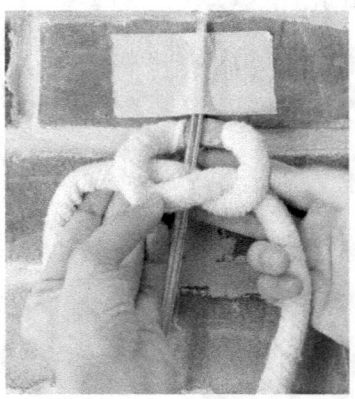

6. Pull the whole cord length through the little created loop located on the left part of the lamp wire.

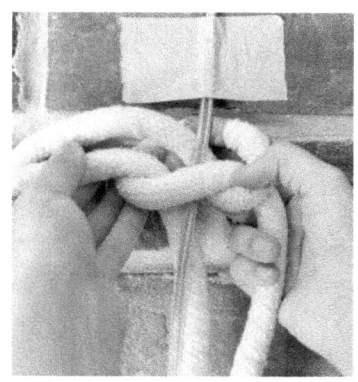

7. Continue repeating this process and your design will begin to change to a spiral one. If you are beginning from the left part, take it on the top of the lamp wire to make the spiral move in a similar pathway. Additionally, if you take the right part on the top or place it on the left part below the spiral, the directions of the spiral will be altered and you will need to lose the knots.

8. After completing your entire knots, you can now proceed to wire the socket. This process can be done before knotting.

9. To make a socket cover, you need to get a planter or cup. Then get a driller and make a hole in the lower part of the cup. Furthermore, join the threaded nipple to the underside of the socket and ensure it is tightened enough so that it won't lose when putting the light bulb.

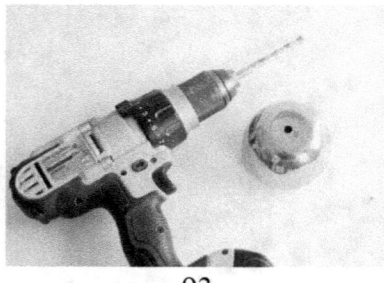

10. From there, you can place the washer, cup, and socket base on the lamp wire. Look at the given instructions and join the socket as you are told.

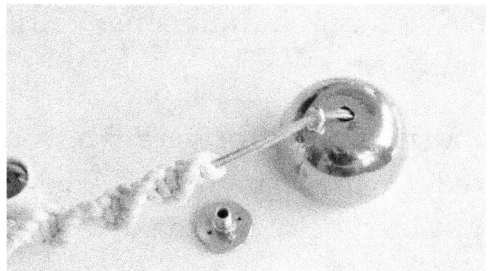

Finally, screw the washer on the threaded nipple and move your rope upwards around the edge of the threaded nipple before applying glue.

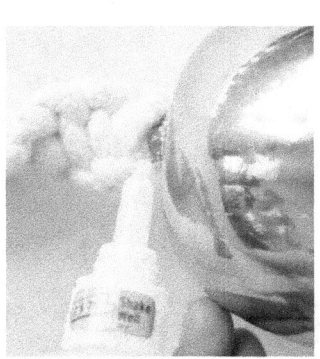
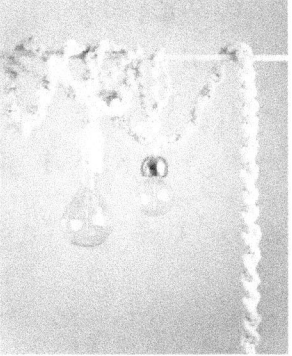

Macramé Christmas Tree

The Christmas season is a time to show love and help one another from their sad moments and you can easily do this by making a macramé Christmas tree and gifting them.

Making one is straightforward and easy, and it also does not require too many tools. A beginner can follow the steps outlined below to make a macramé Christmas tree.

Supplies

- Fishing line for hanging
- Cord, wool or yarn
- Comb or brush
- Jewelry wire
- Some straight twigs

Instructions

1. To begin this process, cut the yarn into 8 inches of different pieces.
2. Then pick up two of the cut strands and wrap them in half to create a loop. Afterwards, position one of the loops below a twig.

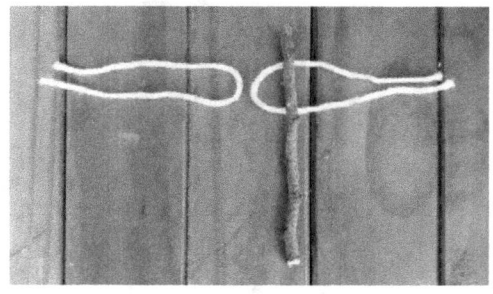

3. Use the looped edge of the other strand and push the ends of the strand below the twig through the loop. Thread the strand's ends and tighten properly.

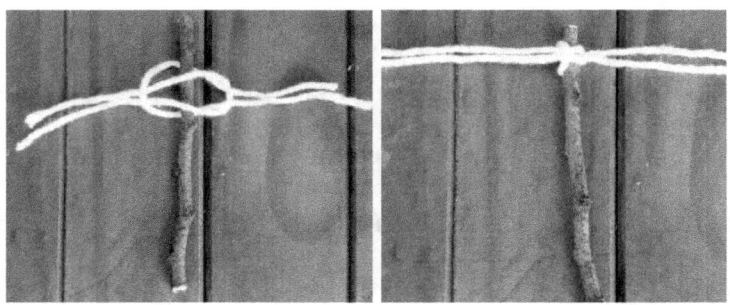

4. Repeat the process above for other pieces of yarn for about ¾ of the twig, then use a brush to spread the strands

Macramé Table Runner

A macramé table runner is perfect for placing tea cups and flower vases on. You can create one using easy knots. Looking to begin your macramé journey? Look no further than the macramé table runner.

Supplies

- Scissors
- 12" wooden dowel
- 2" cotton twine for a dowel hanger
- Over the door hooks
- 22 strands of 16" cotton rope measuring about 3mm

Instructions

1. Tie the cotton twine to every end of your wooden dowel and hang it from the top of your door kooks. Then wrap your first 16" rope strand in half and make a lark's head knot on the top of your dowel.

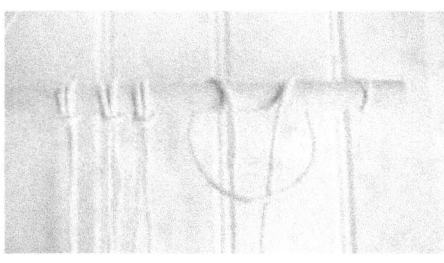

2. Keep on adding each 16" strand of rope with a lark's head knot until you amass 22. As a result, it will total up to 44 strands.

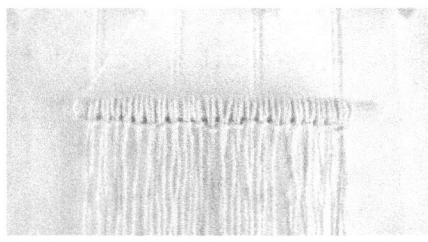

3. The next step requires you to pull the outside right rope over the front of the entire ropes and

wrap the end over your door hook. This process will serve as the bottom for the subsequent row of knots known as half-hitch that will form a horizontal row. Use the second rope from the right-hand side to tie the only knot around the rope you folded across. This will make it under 6" the dowel.

4. With a similar strand, proceed to tie a second knot on the top-bottom strand. This is known as a half-hitch knot.

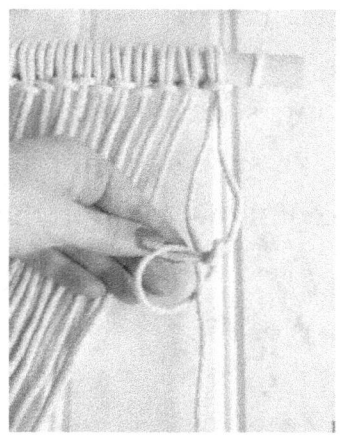

5. Ensure they are leveled. Go through the same step for the second, third, and fourth rope from the outer side and also tie a second half-hitch knot. At this point, you will begin to see the pattern and this is called horizontal half-hitch.

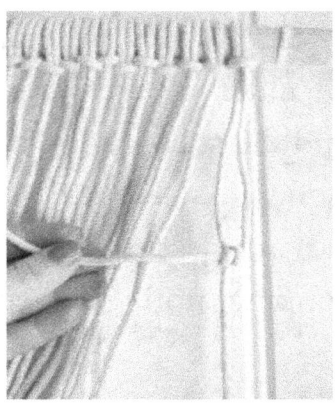

6. Keep on tying successive ropes in one knot all through. Make sure you don't make this process very tight to pull the width in the entire ends.

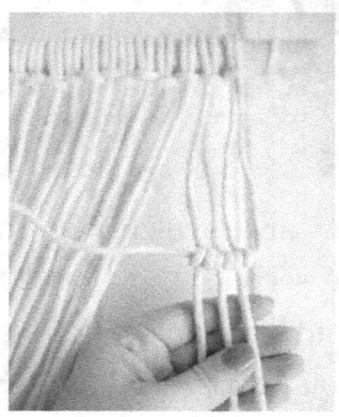

7. Beginning from the right-hand side, make use of the outside four strands and make a square knot around 1.5" under your horizontal line of knots. Move beyond the subsequent four strands and tie a second square knot with 9 strands until 12. Keep on moving past four, and tie four strands without stopping until you achieve what you want.

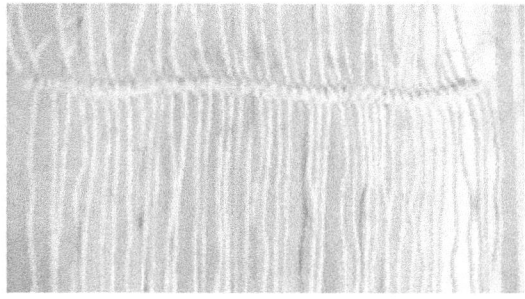

8. Beginning from the right part once more, utilize the four strands you moved past previously and tie a square knot around 3" under the dowel.

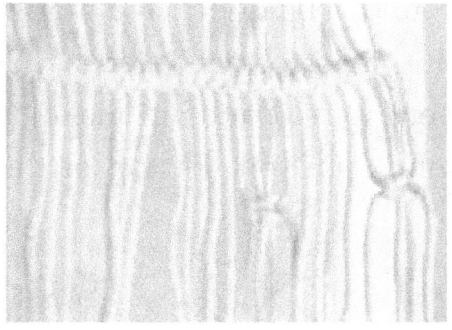

9. Continue tying the skipped four strands in square knots until the row is completed.

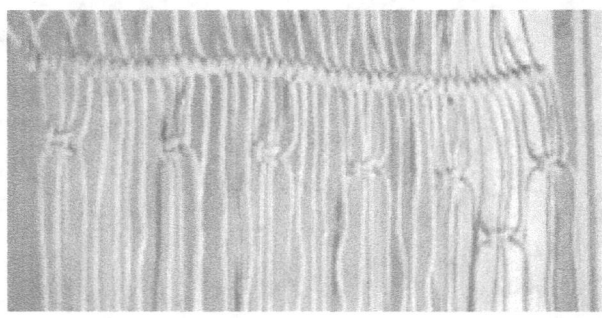

10. Next, pull the outside two strands on the right-hand side to the other side. Afterward, use 3 strands all through 6 to make a different square knot around 11" under the horizontal row of knots in the former steps. Also, use the subsequent four strands to make another square knot around 1.5" on the top of the final square knot.

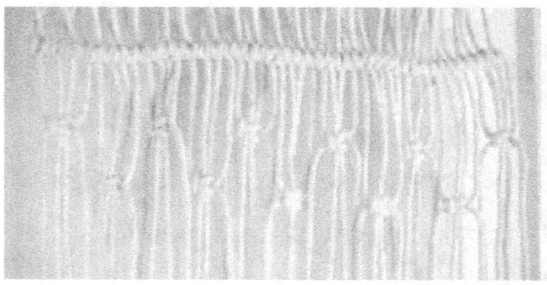

11. Keep on moving across the strands and do not touch the final two strands.

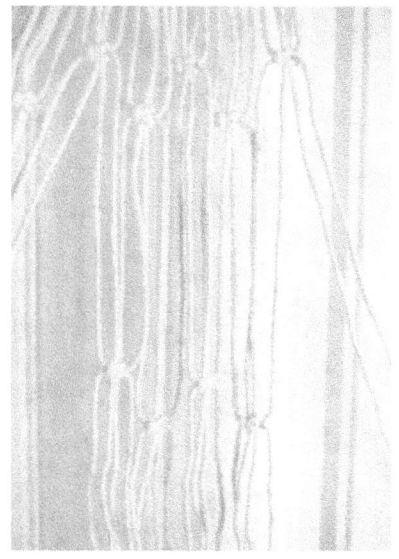

12. Beginning from the right side once more, make another row of horizontal half-hitch knots by going through from the third step to the seventh step, as seen below.

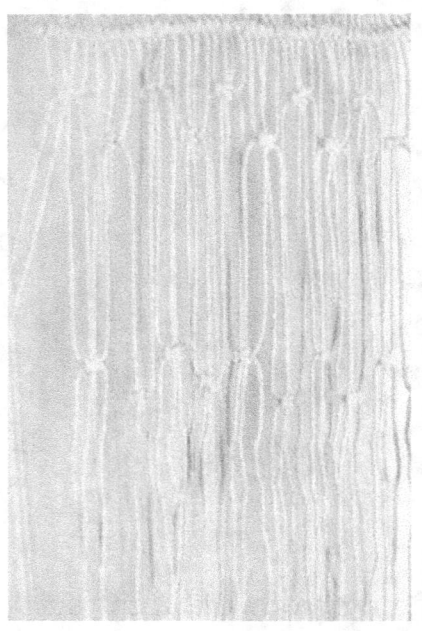

13. Moving over from the left-hand side, utilize a similar bottom strand of rope and make a new horizontal half-hitch row of knots around 2.5" under the final one. In this stop, you will need to work from the left-hand side to the right-hand side.

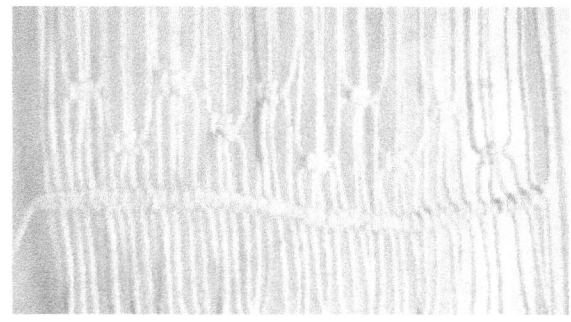

14. Still on the left-hand side, make a row of square knots and do not move past any strands that are on 1" under the horizontal line of knots. Proceed to make the second row of square knots by moving past the initial two strands on the left-hand side before tying a new row of square knots. This process is referred to as an alternating square knot. While doing this, ensure you don't leave too much gap between the rows, so you can always pull them firmly together while adding each square knot.

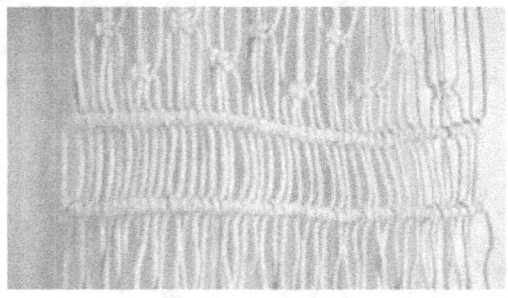

15. Continue moving until you achieve around 13 rows of alternating square knots total. This part will serve as the middle of your table runner.

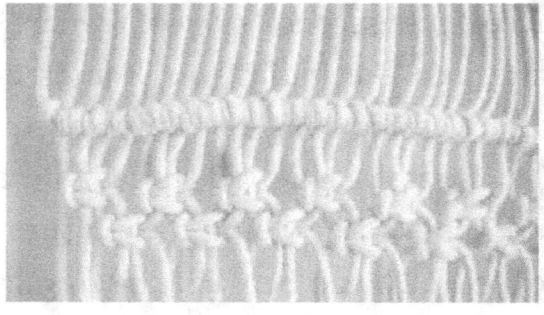

16. In this step, you can add a new horizontal half-hitch row of knots from the outside left-hand side and move towards the right-hand side.

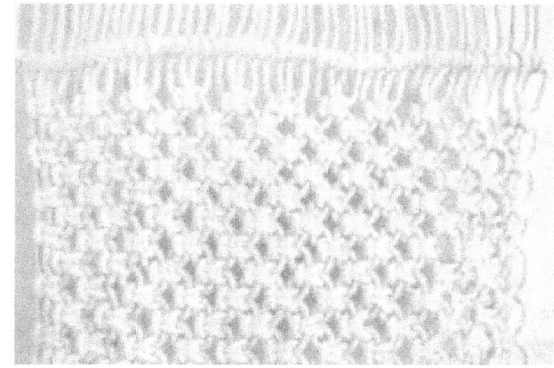

17. Go down around 2.5" and utilize a similar base rope to make a new horizontal half-hitch row of knots that cut across from the right-hand side to the left-hand side.

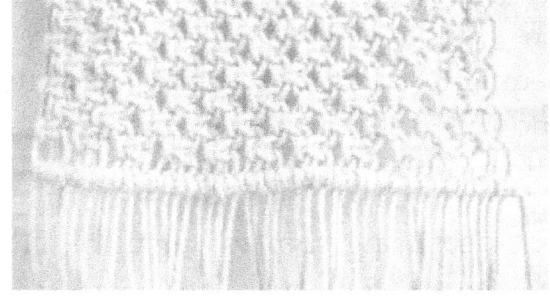

18. Move past the outside two strands of rope situated on the right-hand side and proceed to tie a square knot with strands 3 through 6. Also, move past strands 7 through 10 and utilize

strands 11 through 14 to tie a new square knot. Go through this process again and make sure you are moving past four strands. In the end, you will get 6 strands on the left-hand side.

Move past rows one and two on the left-hand side and further tie strands 3 through 6 into a square knot around 1.5" under the final row of square knots. Proceed to move past the subsequent 4 strands and end the pattern for the second row of square knots. Thus, you will have 6 additional strands on the right-hand side.

19. Use a measuring tool to calculate 11" from the final row of horizontal knots and tie a square knot with the outside 4 strands on the right-hand side. You should then tie the subsequent 4 into a square knot around 1.5" over the final knot.

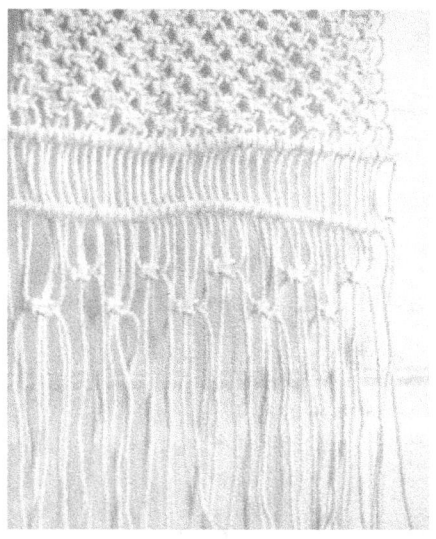

20. Repeat the entire steps once more and move to the final step.

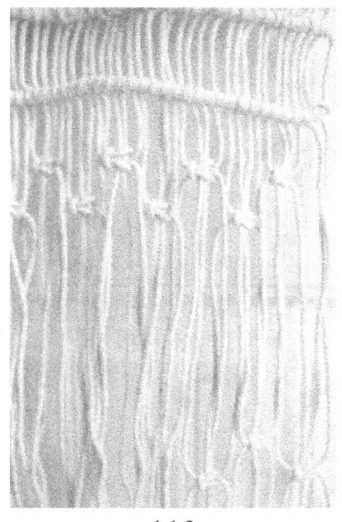

21. In the final step, tie a row of horizontal half-hitch knots around 1.5" underneath the row of changing square knots. Then cut the ends of the knots to make it long as you want, creating notes of how lengthy the knots stay on the other end. Take away the cotton twine from your dowel and slide the entire lark's head knots slowly. Lastly, trim the middle of the lark's head knot loop and cut the ends.

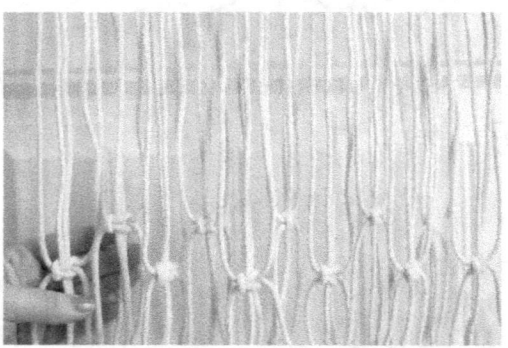

22. There you have it; you have successfully made your macramé table runner.

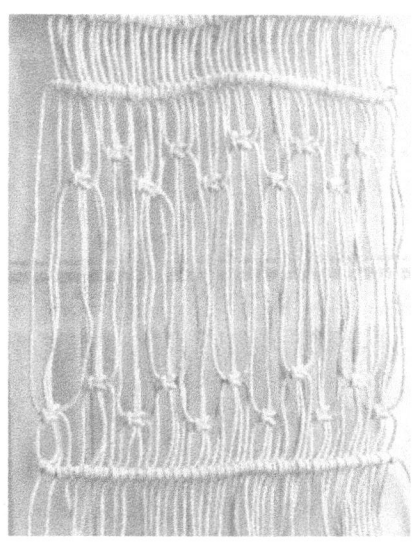

Double Macramé Plant Holder

Making a single macramé plant holder might be easy, but making the one that has several layers is much more challenging. Meanwhile, as a beginner, you can kick-start your macramé journey by making a plant holder with multiple levels.

Supplies

- A ruler
- Glue
- 3 Ceramic bowls

- Scissors
- 30 yards of rope
- Attractive plants

Instructions

1. Begin the process of making macramé plant holders by making a rope to hold your 3 ceramic bowls. Then proceed to cut 8 pieces of ripe 30 inches for every rope.
2. Create a knot at one edge, which will help in holding the 8 pieces together. Meanwhile, ensure you do not forget to make it tight.

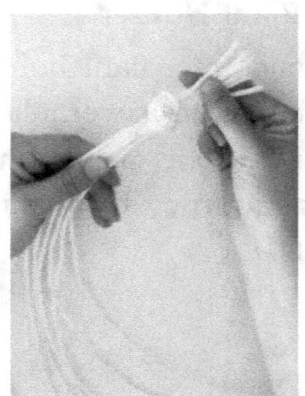

3. Pick up a bowl and position it upside down and place the knot on the middle before

differentiating the 8 strings 2 by 2 to create a cross shape.

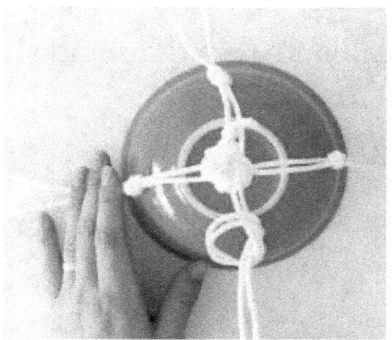

4. Create a knot, around 3 inches from the middle, which will hold every pair of strings firmly.

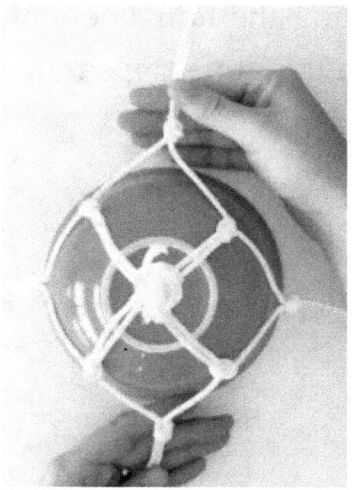

5. Pick up a single string from each pair and attach them with a knot. Afterward, the rope in the middle of the first and second knot rows will automatically create a diamond shape.

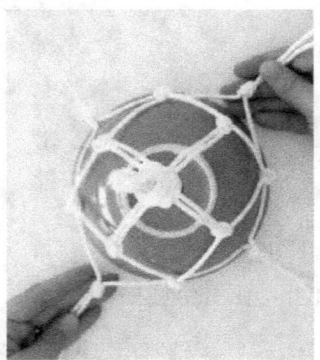

6. After creating the four knots of the second row, go through the same steps to make the third row of four knots.

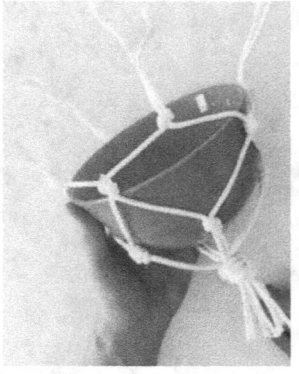

7. Supposing you are using the usual cereal bowl, you are expected only to use three rows of knots to hold the bowl firmly. Also, ensure the rope holder is large to hold the bowl well.

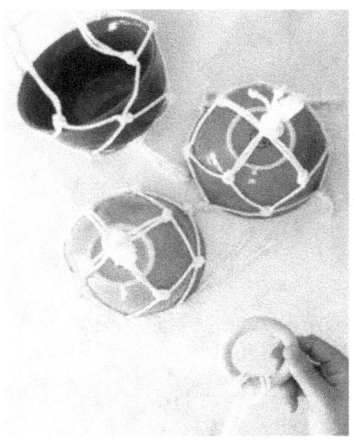

8. Go through the former steps once more to make rope support for the three bowls.

9. The next step requires you to join your entire bowl support together to make your hanging planter. Next, cut two pieces of rope of 3 yards. Then wrap them in the center and create a loop using them, going through the rope and in the

wooden ring. As a result, you need to have 4 strings of 1 ½ yard hanging from around the ring.

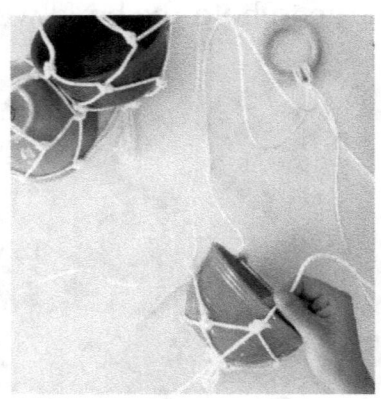

10. Join each string using a knot that was tied to the initial rope support. Endeavor to get a similar distance between the ring and the different knots you create. To make your process flawless, you should take up a rule and sketch a small mark on each of the ropes at a space of 25 inches from around the ring. This process is vital, especially if you want your ceramic bowl planters to stay horizontally.
11. Proceed to join the second and the third support underneath the initial one, allowing a little gap of

around 12 inches between the second and third support. Also, cut the additional rope length of each knot if needed and include little glue. Once the planter is watering, it will stop the knot from slipping.

12. Place your plants back into the bowls. If you can't find a drain hole, it is important to include a few pebbles below before placing the soil and plant.

13. Finally, you have to drill a hole in the ceiling and screw a hook. With the wooden ring, ensure you hand your rope planter and position your bowls planters into every rope support. There you have it, you have successfully made a plant holder with multiple layers.

Macramé Feathers

The soothing effect of the macramé feathers cannot be overemphasized. Placing the feathers on our body gives us a sense of calmness and a feeling of excitement.

Furthermore, the macramé feather is a simple and easy-to-do macramé project for beginners and professionals as well.

Supplies

- A ruler
- Fabric stiffener

- Cat brush
- 5mm one twist cotton string
- Sharp fabric shears

Instructions

1. If you are using a medium feature size, cut the following:
    - 1 32" strand meant for the spine area
    - 10-12 14" strands meant for the top area
    - 8-10 12" strands meant for the center area
    - 6-8 10" strands meant for the lower area

In this same step, ensure you wrap 32" strand in half. Then pick up one of the 14" strands and wrap it in half before putting it below the spine.

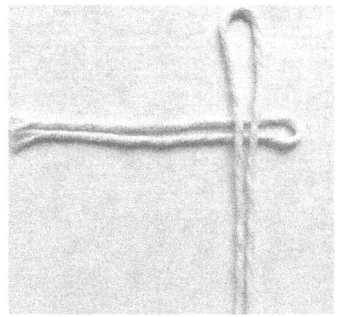

2. Pick up a new 14" strand, wrap it in half and place it inside the loop of the upper horizontal strand. Ensure you pull it and position it horizontally, on the upper part of the other strand.

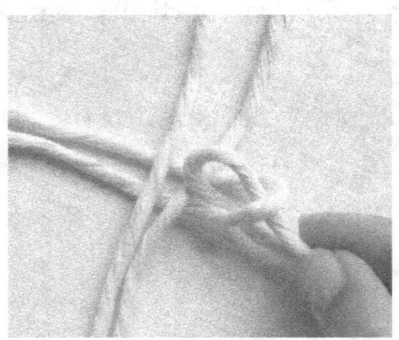

3. Afterward, pull the lower strands and stop at the upper loop. This will serve as your knot.

4. Gently pull the two sides firmly. On the subsequent row, you will have to change the

starting part. This means that if you positioned it horizontally from the left side to the right side initially, you need to position the horizontal strand from the right part to the left side.

5. Place the initially wrapped strand below the spine, and thread a new wrapped strand into the loop. Subsequently, ensure you pull the bottom strands through the upper loop before you tighten it.

6. Continue working your way slowly in size.
7. Ensure you push the strands to make sure it is tightened. Then take the lower spine strand using a single hand and another strand using your other hand before pushing the strands upwards. After doing so, draw the fringe to the lower side to reach the under of the center strand.

8. Proceed to present a rough cut. This will help it shape well and also brush the strands out. If the strands are short, it will be easier to cut. Additionally, it helps to create a sharp pair of fabric shears

9. Once done with the rough cut, lay the feather on a long-lasting and resilient surface while you start using an animal brush to bush the rope. Be aware that the brush will ruin any soft or word surface. To avoid damaging the soft or wooden surface, ensure you get an even cardboard box or a self-healing cutting mat.

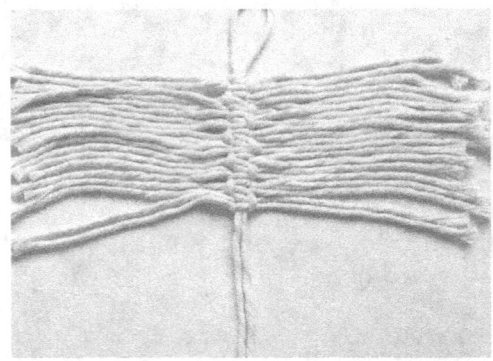

10. Whenever you begin brushing the rope, begin at the spine and move hard into the rope. Be aware that it will require some hard strokes to derive the amazing soft fringe you want.

11. Keep on working all the way down. Once you get below, grab the bottom of the spine as you brush and ensure the brush does not ruin any strands.

12. Subsequently, you need to make the feather much harder. The rope is very soft that it will ruin if you drag it and attempt to hand it. To avoid this, spray it and leave it to dry for some hours.

13. After waiting for like 4 hours, your feather will become harder and you are now free to return to work and give it the last trim. This will be the most difficult aspect of the macramé feather. You don't need to rush this process because you might end up damaging it entirely. Instead, be patient because you may have to change your trim depending on how regularly you are changing the position of the piece. After cutting short the feather, you are still free to give it a new stray of fabric stiffener to offer an amazing size. Once done, you are now free and ready to hang in your completed macramé feather project.

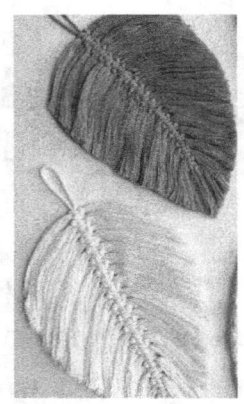

Macramé Ornaments

If the festive season is approaching, the mini macramé Christmas ornaments are the perfect choice of decoration in homes and other places. Unsurprisingly, it is a beginner-friendly type of design meant to get people into the Christmas season.

Supplies

- Twigs
- Scissors
- Macramé cord/rope
- Comb or hairbrush
- Masking tape

Instructions

1. To begin making a mini macramé Christmas ornament, you need to cut a little twig and utilize the lark's head knot to join six cords to the upper part. While doing this, ensure that each cord should take the form of about 2 feet.

2. If you want to tie a lark's head knot, endeavor to wrap the cord in half and proceed to tie the center of the cord on the upper part of the twig.

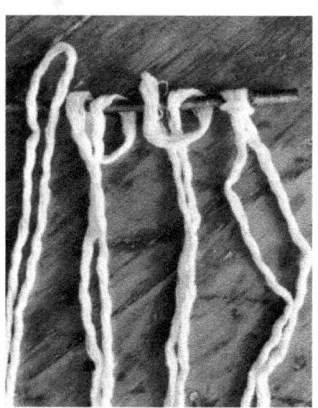

3. Also, wrap the loop on the top of the rear side of the twig before pulling the two edges through the

loop. While doing so, pull it tightly and repeat the same steps for the entire 6 cords.

Making square knot mini macramé Christmas ornament

Frist Square Knot

Whenever the cords are over the twig, you should begin with the first row, serving as the three square knots. The knots are wrapped with 4 cords. This means you need to begin on the left-hand side and divide the other first 4 cords.

To form the square knot, use the left-hand cord and pull it to resemble the number 4 shape. Subsequently, put the end of the first cord below the fourth cord.

Afterward, take out the end of the fourth cord over and at the back of the center two cords and through the gap between the first and second cord that resembles the fourth cord.

Then pull the edges of the first and fourth cord and ensure they are both tightened and taken to the top. You can make it the first half of the square knot.

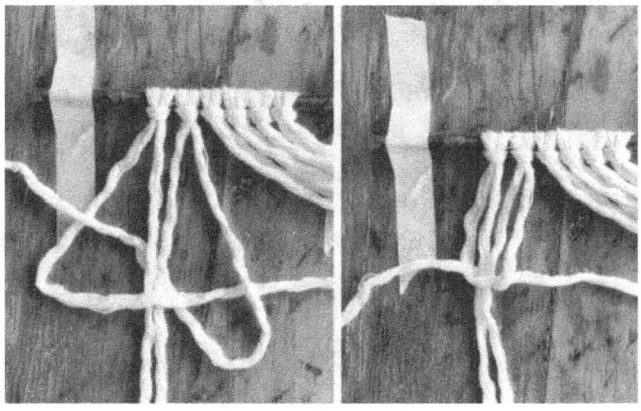

To get the second half of the square knot, you will have to carry out a similar task, though it will come in the other direction. In this step, you will allow your four shaped design with the first and fourth cord; however, the fourth one will face the right-hand side.

Proceed to pull the first cord on the top of the fourth one before placing the tail of the first cord below the second and third cord and on the top of the space of the fourth shape.

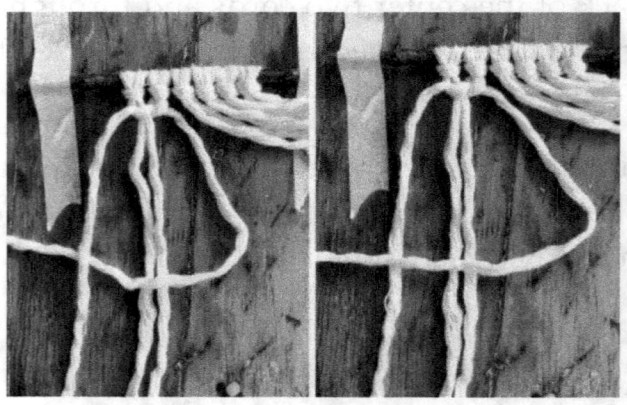

Finally, pull the ends of the first and fourth cord to make them tighten, and you have achieved your first square knot.

How to get the first 3 Rows

To get your first 3 rows, you are advised to continue working in parts of the four cords. Then proceed to tie a new square knot and another one to create a 3 along the upper row.

To get the 2nd row, you will only need to create the second square knots. To achieve this, divide the first cord, and follow it by the subsequent four cords, which will act as the second square knot on the second row before the subsequent one again.

As a result, the other two cords will be on the other end as well. To get the third and final row, endeavor to use the middle four cords of the tow to wrap a single square knot. At this point, you will need to ensure all knots are evenly tightened and given enough gap.

To make the fourth row, go through the same steps for row 2 alongside the 2 square knots, ignoring the two cords on both sides.

Meanwhile, for the fifth row, go through the first row alongside the 3 square knots.

How to get the half hitch knot (Row 6)

You can round up this mini macramé Christmas ornament design with square knots or add a row of half hitch knots.

If you decide to add a row of half hitch knots, you can do so by following the step-by-step guide below:

1. Pick up the first cord in the row before pulling it across the mini macramé Christmas ornament horizontally (this will be your first and leading cord).

2. Pick up the second cord from the back and on the top of the first cord through the gap you made.

3. Continue for the other cords, and still ensure the first cord is placed across horizontally and even while bending the other cords close to it.

4. Finally, conclude by tightening the knots; just make sure you pull the first cord.

Conclude this macramé design

To conclude this design, ensure you cut the edges or cut it into a down or up "V" shape below. Next, utilize a comb or hairbrush to brush the cord and make the fringe underside. At this point, you may have to trim the shape once more after brushing it out.

Last, of all, cut the edges of the twig and include a piece of cord to hang the ornament successfully.

Chapter 6

Common Macramé Mistakes to Avoid

Here are some of the common macramé mistakes you need to avoid when creating any project:

1. Not purchasing sufficient cord

As a macramé project designer, you need to ensure you buy enough cord for your projects. You wouldn't like to run out of cords when creating a macramé project during the weekends or at night.

It would be a terrible experience and it is something that you should endeavor to avoid. For most people, not having enough cord will surely damage or ruin their planned macramé project.

To ensure you will purchase enough cord, you may have to calculate the required length needed. For instance, when you decide to make a wall hanger, you will need to measure diagonally and through the stick. Furthermore, each cord needs to use about ½ inch across the stick, so this needs to be factored in your calculation.

From the explanation above, you will determine the number of strands you will use, and from there, you can calculate the length that each strand will have.

2. **Cutting the cord very short**

This is one of the common mistakes experienced by most macramé designers. It is one thing to purchase enough cord and it is another thing to cut the cord to the perfect size or slightly above the right size.

Even if you have enough cord, you still need to learn to cut the cord to the right size if at all you want to make an exceptional macramé project. Cutting the cord very short will leave your project ruined and unfinished.

Here's a tip: Ensure you cut the cord about 4x the length of your projected design. Additionally, if you will be wrapping your cord in half, it needs to be about 8x the length of the project.

3. **Learn and keep on practicing knots**

Although many people may not agree that this is a macramé mistake, it is indeed one. Learning and continuing to practice knots should be taken seriously if you seek to avoid mistakes in your macramé project.

Imagine making your first macramé project and you are making a series of mistakes with the knots; how would you feel? Bad, I guess. So, to not make the mistake of not being able to knot properly, practicing should be a constant hobby.

Nonetheless, if you are unaware of how to go about making the knots as a beginner, you can simply pick up a stick and some 3-foot strands of cords and begin practicing with the aid of the several knots discussed in the beginning chapters of this book until you are confident of your abilities.

Once you become comfortable with tying the knots, you can proceed with your macramé projects. But when you begin your projects, do not focus mainly on the knots; carry on your project like you are already an expert and you will be shocked at the amazing projects you will create.

4. Pulling the knots not too tight and very tight

When making a macramé project, you need to ensure you are pulling the knots tight because it needs to stay without removing. However, if you manage to pull the knots too tight (mostly on a two-half-hitch knot), it is likely to twist your macramé project on its back.

On the other hand, because you are trying to ensure you are not pulling your knots too tight, you may pull your knots not tight enough, making your project not good enough. You need to balance pulling your knots too tight and not too tight.

In this case, the best thing to do is to continue with similar tightness all through your macramé project, but if it begins to curl, ensure you lose it a bit.

This is one trick that has worked for many macramé projects and they will work for you also if your concentration level is high because you will need to be watchful whenever the knots begin to curl.

5. Letting go

Assuming your first macramé project does not go as planned, it can be very alluring to let it go and move on with other aspects of life. But as they say, no good thing comes easy, so why should you give up?

Most macramé designers had a very bad project on their first attempt, but they slowly grew to create stunning projects by consistently learning and practicing.

Getting equipped with the right information, tips, tricks, and techniques will set you on your way to creating awesome macramé projects. You should have a "don't give up" attitude if you want to be a successful macramé crafter.

Once you have mastered the art (which can even come in your 10th project), macramé will become an interesting art that you will find joy doing.

The end… almost!

Hey! We've made it to the final chapter of this book, and I hope you've enjoyed it so far.

If you have not done so yet, I would be incredibly thankful if you could take just a minute to leave a quick review on Amazon

Reviews are not easy to come by, and as an independent author with a little marketing budget, I rely on you, my readers, to leave a short review on Amazon.

Even if it is just a sentence or two!

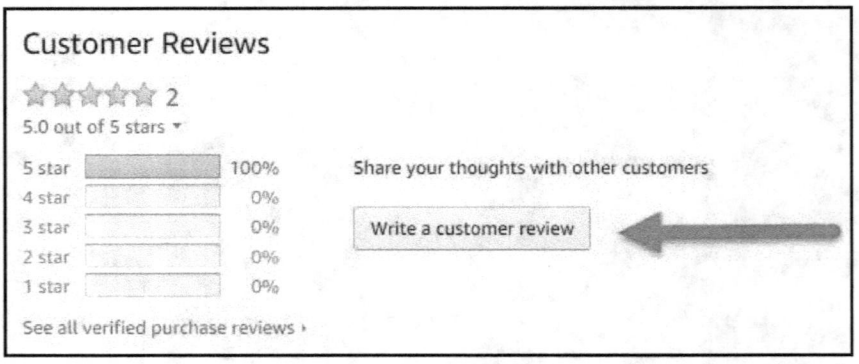

So if you really enjoyed this book, please…

>> Click here to leave a brief review on Amazon.

I truly appreciate your effort to leave your review, as it truly makes a huge difference.

Chapter 7

Macramé Frequently Asked Questions (FAQs)

Perhaps you just started your macramé journey and you are still learning, you may want to check out what other beginners are also asking.

The most frequently asked questions about macramé are outlined below:

1. **What is the difference between a cord and rope?**

Ans – The difference between a cord and rope is not so much noticeable. However, a cord is an all-encompassing term that is usually used to refer to several materials that have long strands. These lengthy strands may not necessarily be woven, twisted, or braided.

On the other hand, the rope is classified under the group of cord and it features multiple fibers that are braided, twisted, and woven together to form a working cord.

2. **What kind of materials is needed for macramé projects?**

Ans – The kind of materials you need for your macramé project is dependent on the type of design you want to achieve. You should ask yourself different questions, including what type of macramé project you want to create? Is the project for outdoor or indoor purposes? And so much more.

For the second question, if you are creating a macramé project for indoor purposes, you can use cotton, while if it for outdoor purposes, you need to ensure you use a weather-resistant material such as polypropylene rope.

Other questions you can ask yourself include if the project is a practical or decorative one. If it is a practical one, you can use a sturdy and thick rope, while a decorative project may require you to use a fragile material. Such deep questions will help you discover what you need for your project and help you weigh your options correctly.

Also, the size of your completed macramé project will assist you in knowing the diameter of your string or rope. For example, if you want to make a 6 foot by 10-foot wedding arbor, you will have to use a 5mm rope that forms a large knot, saving you time and the knots for later use.

Finally, the material you should utilize for your macramé project should be based on your taste and style. For instance, you can choose a colorful material or texture you like while making your preferred macramé project.

3. **How can I hang my work when knotting?**

Ans – A portable and convenient closet bar and clothing rack can be used to hang your work when knotting. For example, you can hang some S hooks from the closet bar and leave your dowel from the hooks before joining your knotting cords to the dowel.

4. **What is macramé made of?**

Ans – This is one of the common questions asked by most macramé beginners. Macramé is made of anything (object or item) you can tie a knot to make. These objects or items may include leather, shoelaces, rubber cording, cloth strips, paracord, yarn, and others.

Meanwhile, macramé majorly consists of string or rope and the things that the string or rope is made of. Some of the things contained in strings or ropes include linen, wool, cotton, hemp, and jute.

5. What is the quantity of rope that should be cut for a macramé project?

Ans – The most important thing to know in this aspect is to cut your cord 4 times your preferred length of your completed macramé project.

For example, if you want to wrap the cord in half, you need to make it 8 times the length of your completed macramé project. So, always make sure you get more than enough quantity of rope you need for your macramé project. It will save you from running out of cord or rope when making a macramé project.

6. Can I learn macramé easily?

Ans – Yes. Macramé is an easy craft to learn. All you need to do is to learn everything about it, practice it extensively, and go ahead to make your first macramé project. While learning the craft, ensure you are committed and practice without the fear of not getting it right. The practicing aspect should be taken seriously and be sure you are patient during the process of making macramé crafts.

7. What type of cord is needed for a macramé project?

Ans – The type of cord you need is dependent on the macramé project you want to make. You are allowed to use the different types of rope or strings for your macramé project.

Some people are known to use a clothesline, yarn, and jute for their macramé project, any of which is fine. For others, their best cord for making macramé projects is the 4mm three-strand macramé cord.

8. **Can macramé be tagged as crochet?**

Ans – A lot of people often get confused when macramé and crochet are compared. Although both deal with textiles; however, the techniques and processes involved are entirely different.

While macramé uses complex and intricate hitch and knot to make patterns, crochet uses needles alongside loops of yarn. Another difference between both crafts is that macramé is mostly used for home decoration while crochet is used for clothing.

Conclusion

Macramé is a craft, which when you have a mastery of, will be very beneficial to you, i.e., you will be able to create several art pieces like the ones discussed in the pages of this book and more, and guess what? You also have the opportunity of selling them for profit.

This book, broken down into step-wise chapters, I believe, has helped you answer most if not all of the questions you had in mind and has given you virtually all you need to confidently get started with making awesome macramé designs and become a PRO in no time.

Hence, I hope you found this beginner's guide enlightening and fun at the same time. I would love to hear your thoughts in the review section on Amazon but until then…

Happy knotting, crafters!

www.ingramcontent.com/pod-product-compliance
Lightning Source LLC
Chambersburg PA
CBHW050322120526
44592CB00014B/2018